CAMPAIGN 435

DONBAS 2014–15

Undeclared and Uncivil War in Ukraine

MARK GALEOTTI

ILLUSTRATED BY MARC LEE

OSPREY PUBLISHING
Bloomsbury Publishing Plc
Kemp House, Chawley Park, Cumnor Hill, Oxford OX2 9PH, UK
Bloomsbury Publishing Ireland Limited,
29 Earlsfort Terrace, Dublin 2, D02 AY28, Ireland
Bloomsbury Publishing Inc.
1359 Broadway, 12th Floor, New York, NY 10018, USA
E-mail: info@ospreypublishing.com
www.ospreypublishing.com

OSPREY is a trademark of Osprey Publishing Ltd

First published in Great Britain in 2026

A catalogue record for this book is available from the British Library.

ISBN: PB 9781472868473; eBook 9781472868480; ePDF 9781472868459; XML 9781472868466

26 27 28 29 30 10 9 8 7 6 5 4 3 2 1

Maps by Bounford.com
3D BEVs by Paul Kime
Index by Alan Rutter
Typeset by Lumina Datamatics Ltd
Printed by Repro India Ltd

Osprey Publishing supports the Woodland Trust, the UK's leading woodland conservation charity.

MIX
Paper
FSC FSC® C047271

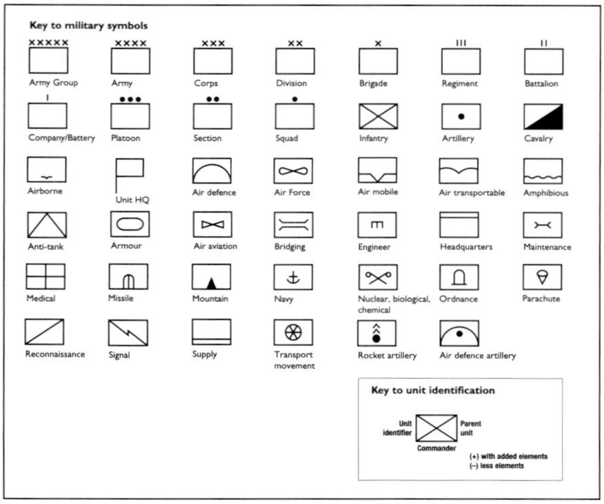

Author's note

Translating out of foreign alphabets always poses challenges. I have chosen to transliterate names as they are pronounced, and have also ignored the diacritical 'soft' and 'hard' signs found in the original Cyrillic. I will generally use the Ukrainian form for Ukrainian locations, even when not under Kyiv's control (so Odesa instead of Odessa, Luhansk instead of Lugansk), but for people's and entities' names, the individuals' preferred forms are used. That does inevitably mean that, for example, the capital of the Lugansk People's Republic is Luhansk.

There are also political minefields in deciding what to call the fighters in the east. They were by no means all secessionists, many were anti-Kyiv more than pro-Moscow, and so on. I use terms such as militant, rebel, anti-Maidan and anti-government fairly interchangeably, not least simply to vary the text and make it more readable.

Abbreviations

AA	Anti-air
Abn	Airborne
AFV	Armoured fighting vehicle
AGL	Automatic grenade launcher
APC	Armoured personnel carrier
AT	Anti-tank
ATO	Anti-Terrorist Operation
Bde	Brigade
Bn	Battalion
BTG	Battalion tactical group
Col.	Colonel
Coy	Company
Div	Division
DNR	*Donetskaya Narodnaya Respublika*: Donetsk People's Republic
DPSU	*Derzhavna prykordonna sluzhba Ukrainy*: State Border Guard Service (Ukraine)
FSB	*Federalnaya sluzhba bezopasnosti:* Federal Security Service (Russian domestic security agency)
Gen.	General
GU	*Glavnoye upravleniye*: Main Directorate of the General Staff (Russian military intelligence – still widely known by old acronym GRU)
IFV	Infantry fighting vehicle
LNR	*Luganskaya Narodnaya Respublika*: Lugansk People's Republic
Lt.	Lieutenant
Maj.	Major
MANPADS	Man-Portable Air Defence System
Mech	Mechanized
MLRS	Multiple-Launch Rocket System
Mot Inf	Motorized infantry
MR	Motor rifle
MVS	*Ministerstvo vnutrishnikh sprav*: Ministry of Internal Affairs (Ukrainian)
OUN	Organization of Ukrainian Nationalists
Rgt	Regiment
RPG	Rocket-propelled grenade (launcher)
SBU	*Sluzhba bezpeky Ukrainy*: Security Service of Ukraine
SPG	Self-propelled gun
TDB	Territorial defence battalion (Ukrainian)
ZSU	*Zbroiny sili Ukraini*: Ukrainian Armed Forces

Front cover main illustration: The battle for Vuhlehirsk, 28 January 2015. (Marc Lee)
Title page photograph: Government troops ride a BTR APC during a mission to clear rebel roadblocks outside Sloviansk in April 2014. (Photo by Pierre Crom/Getty Images)

CONTENTS

ORIGINS OF THE CAMPAIGN

The emerging and undeclared struggle for Ukraine's south-eastern Donbas region, which erupted after the Russian annexation of Crimea in February–March 2014 and only effectively froze in mid-2015 with the Minsk II peace deal, was at once an insurgency, a proxy war and a direct Russian intervention. At first, it was a struggle largely between local insurgents and Russian volunteers on the one hand, local security forces and pro-government militias on the other. Some of these revolts fizzled out, some were suppressed, some created the basis for self-declared 'people's republics'. Initially, Moscow was unimpressed, but by summer 2014, it had decided to back the separatists with direct interventions by its own troops, as it began to look as if the new government in Kyiv would be able to reassert control over the Donbas. The next year saw back-and-forth struggles as neither side was able to assert

In many ways, this campaign started looking like a war of irregulars against irregulars. Some rough-and-ready Ukrainian paratroopers in a GAZ-66 utility vehicle mounting a DShK 12.7mm heavy machine gun lead a convoy through the Simonovka neighbourhood of the formerly rebel-held town of Sloviansk. (Photo by Scott Peterson/Getty Images)

A mixed force of DNR rebels and Russian regulars during the 2015 Debaltseve campaign; Russian intervention would transform the conflict and prevent Kyiv from being able to restore its control across the Donbas. (Photo by Pierre Crom/ Getty Images)

itself, until the conflict settled into an uneasy, bad-tempered, on-and-off and ultimately unsustainable stalemate. In this respect, the undeclared war in the Donbas could be considered the first act in the tragic drama that would become the 2022 full-scale invasion of Ukraine.

DONBAS OR DONBASS?

The Donets Coal Basin is a swathe of land in eastern Ukraine that has been defined not just by the Donets River that flows more than 1,000km from across the border in Russia southwards to join the River Don close to the Azov Sea, but also the Donets Ridge highlands sprawling across eastern Ukraine. Either way, the region – contracted to Donbas in Ukrainian, but Donbass in Russian – has long been a borderland. In the 16th to the 18th centuries, it was considered part of the 'Wild Fields', the contested no-man's-land originally raided by slave-taking Tatars from the east and the south. Later, it became the frontier between two great Cossack confederations: the Zaporizhian Sich to the west, and the Don Cossack Host to the east. With the former often connected with the Polish–Lithuanian state and the latter in due course subordinated to Muscovy, Donbas was soon drawn into their wider

The fog of war

All conflicts are, by definition, spun and mythologized, both at the time and subsequently. In the modern internet and social media age, though, this is a particular issue. The widespread availability of information from participants' accounts to satellite photography ought to make everything that much more transparent, but this is offset against the proliferation of mistaken assessments and fake information, industrial-scale misrepresentations and outright 'narrative warfare'. This is a particular problem in a conflict such as this one, which was at once a civil war, a denied and proxy foreign invasion and a political revolution as elites reinvented themselves and supplanted each other. In this context, there will be a greater use of such caveats as 'reportedly' or presentation of rival perspectives on some events, where the facts are not wholly clear. Given just how complex and chaotic this conflict was, frankly everyone should be wary of any accounts, from whatever perspective, that too confidently assert they know the absolute truth…

The Cossacks became mainstays of tsarist Russia's armies. These are a bombardier and a trumpeter of the Don Cossack Life Guards Horse Artillery from 1855, by Karl Piratsky. (Karl Piratsky, public domain, via Wikimedia Commons)

competition, but the 1686 Treaty of Perpetual Peace between Warsaw and Moscow (which, of course, would prove to be nothing of the sort) brought the whole Donbas under Russian rule within what was known as Novorossiya, 'New Russia'. As a result, understandings of just what counted as the Donbas were varied and often contradictory. Some definitions included parts of the neighbouring Russian *oblast* (region) of Rostov, others did not extend to the full boundaries of the Donetsk and Luhansk regions. However, the generally accepted definition became that it primarily comprised these two regions, which in the 19th century would become important sources of coal for both export and to fuel the Russian Empire's belated industrialization.

This was a process that only deepened the degree to which the Donbas would be shaped by a whole mix of cultural influences. Originally settled by runaways, refugees and Cossacks, then moulded by Russian imperial administrators, in the 19th century it welcomed foreign investors and ethnic Russian workers alike. The major city of Donetsk was originally known as Yuzovka after its founder, Welsh businessman John Hughes, who in 1869 began building a coal-mining town on the foundations of Oleksandrivka, an old Cossack settlement. As collieries and metalworks proliferated and railways began to be built, landless peasants from Russia came to work in the new industries. By the end of the 19th century, although the population of the Donbas was still – albeit barely – majority Ukrainian-speaking, Russian-speakers dominated the cities and heavy industry, and continued to grow in number.

Yuzovka at the turn of the century was a grimy but vibrant smokestack city at the heart of Russia's belated industrial revolution. (Unknown photographer of original photo, photocopy created by user:Butko, public domain, via Wikimedia Commons)

The Donbas, 2013

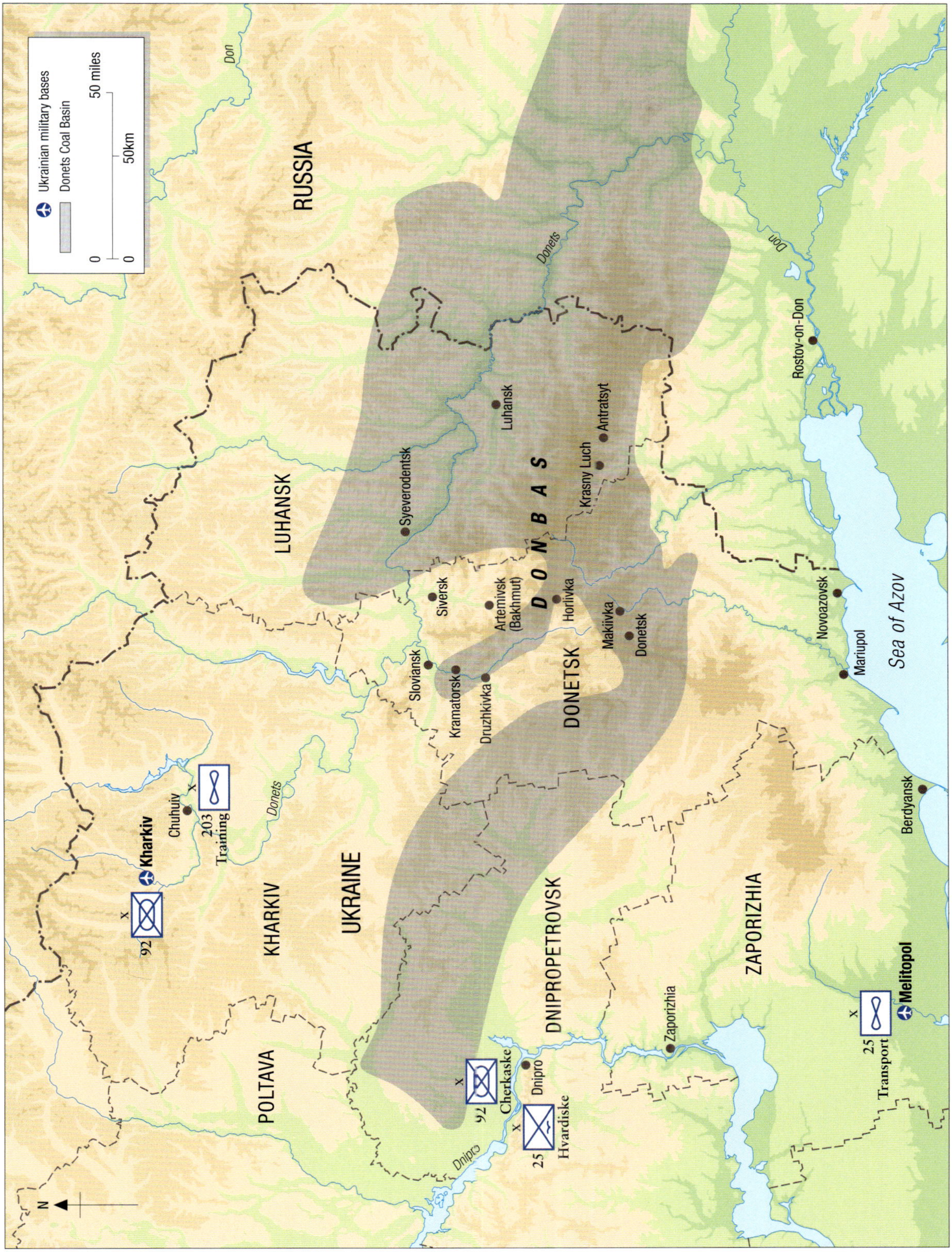

A soldier from the LNR's 2nd Corps, with slung AK-74 rifle. The flag in the background is that of the Don Cossacks, who supplied a substantial number of volunteers for the rebel forces. (Photo by Pierre Crom/ Getty Images)

A CONTESTED REGION

The location and industrial base of the Donbas ensured it would be a strategic target in the conflicted 20th century. In World War I, at first the Russians were able to advance into Austro-Hungarian lands as far as the Carpathian Mountains, but by 1915 they had been checked and forced onto the defensive. They made initial gains in their Brusilov offensive, and arguably could have returned to the attack in 1917, but the tsarist state was about to collapse. The February Revolution saw the tsar deposed and replaced by a Provisional Government with neither the legitimacy nor the authority to meet the challenges ahead of it. The new government was committed to continuing the war, but the army was already crumbling. The Bolshevik Revolution in November 1917 brought a new government to power promising to end the war.

Meanwhile, though, the independent Ukrainian People's Republic was proclaimed, and while this largely excluded the Donbas, nonetheless the next few years would see all of Ukraine become a battleground between competing forces. The Ukrainian War of Independence (1917–21) pitted Bolsheviks, anarchists, Ukrainian nationalists, anti-Bolshevik White Russian forces, Germany and Austria-Hungary, as well as foreign intervention forces, against each other in a multi-directional struggle for supremacy.[1]

In the Donbas, although the Ukrainian People's Republic made some early gains, the self-proclaimed Donetsk–Krivoy Rog Soviet Republic was strong in the industrial cities of the east and represented a powerful ally for the Bolsheviks. However, desperate to end the war, the Bolsheviks signed the Treaty of Brest-Litovsk in March 1918, ceding most of Ukraine to the Central Powers, who proceeded to take the opportunity to push further yet. The Donbas fell to them but, under pressure in the west, they were forced to withdraw, and a new nationalist government, the Directorate, claimed authority over the country. The Bolsheviks were not going to allow the factories, coalfields and grain lands of Ukraine to be lost to them, though, and, in the subsequent Russian Civil War, managed to reconquer it. For the Donbas, this meant a policy of 'decossackization' that would be the prelude to subsequent 'Russification' under Joseph Stalin in the 1930s, with Ukrainian culture undermined and more Russian colonists introduced.

The inter-war period was one of hunger, poverty and terror in the Donbas, as well as crash industrialization. This meant, ironically and tragically, that the Donbas was all the more

A Soviet propaganda poster from 1921 asserting that 'The Donbas is the heart of Russia'. (Rare Book Collection, The New York Public Library)

1 See Men-at-Arms 412, *Ukrainian Armies 1914–55*

important a target for the Germans when they invaded the Soviet Union in 1941. Hitler's priorities were: 'Leningrad first, the Donbas second, Moscow third.' By the end of the year, Donetsk (then called Stalino) and the rest of the Donbas had fallen and was under German military government. Real and suspected partisans were executed, thousands of labourers deported to work in German factories and the region's Jewish population killed outright or sent to concentration camps. In all, some 225,000 civilians would die before 1943, when the Soviets unleashed over a million men in their Donbas offensive and liberated the region. It was ravaged by the war, but its industries were regarded as so strategically vital that it would be a priority for post-war reconstruction.

AFTER THE UNION

The result was further Russification. While ethnic Ukrainians remained the largest group in the Donbas, they would increasingly speak Russian and adopt a Soviet rather than Ukrainian identity. As the USSR lurched towards collapse in the 1980s, Ukrainian nationalism grew, but in the Donbas, this even sparked a counter called the International Movement of Donbass, which campaigned against national independence. Nonetheless, the direction of travel was unstoppable, and when a referendum on independence from the USSR was held at the end of 1991, even in the Luhansk and Donetsk oblasts, more than 83 per cent of voters supported it. When Soviet leader Mikhail Gorbachev formally dissolved the USSR at the end of the year, a new Ukraine was born.

It was a troubled birth, though. The Soviet economy had been designed as a single, integrated machine, and its dissolution broke that machine. Furthermore, the old industries of the Donbas were uneconomic and often highly polluting. By 1993, production was in crisis and average wages had fallen by three-quarters. In response, the miners of the Donbas went on strike, reflecting a growing belief that they were being neglected by Kyiv and had simply exchanged one distant and incompetent government for another. A consultative referendum in 1994 highlighted the growing gap between the Donbas and the rest of the country. Motions on making Russian one of the official state languages of Ukraine and adopting a less centralized, federal governmental structure received the support of over 85 per cent of voters in the Donbas, but failed to pass overall. Although the miners' strike was resolved thanks to economic concessions, there was already a growing rift with the rest of the country.

Nonetheless, there was no serious interest in autonomy, let alone independence. Instead, local disaffection would in due course manifest itself in strong support for the Party of Regions,

The headquarters of today's Security Service of Ukraine (SBU) on Volodymyrska Street in central Kyiv was that of the Ukrainian KGB in Soviet times. (© Mark Galeotti)

The infamous Berkut riot police would eventually be disbanded for their role in suppressing anti-government protests during the Revolution of Dignity. (Ivan Bandura, CC BY 2.0 https://creativecommons.org/licenses/by/2.0, via Wikimedia Commons)

a powerful political machine backed by a number of local business magnates known as oligarchs and a level of corruption that was striking even by Ukrainian standards. In 2010, the Party of Regions endorsed Donetsk-born Viktor Yanukovych and he won the presidential elections that year by a narrow margin, not least thanks to a strong showing in the Donbas. Although they had few illusions about his venality (when he was ousted, his $75 million private estate was found to sport 27 vintage cars, a flock of ostriches and even a solid gold ingot in the shape of a loaf of bread), the people of eastern Ukraine felt that they had one of 'theirs' in Kyiv. Little did they realize that his election would directly lead to revolution and war.

DONBAS AND THE REVOLUTION

Ukraine had, since independence, oscillated between presidents who wanted to see the country more closely aligned with the West and those who instead looked to Russia, which was, after all, its largest single trading partner. Nevertheless, in 2013, Kyiv finished negotiating a free trade and association agreement with the European Union. Initially, Yanukovych supported this, but Moscow, which had originally been relaxed about the agreement, suddenly that summer realized that it would prevent Ukraine from joining its own trade bloc, the Eurasian Economic Union, and could seriously curtail existing economic ties. It began imposing controls on Ukrainian imports, while putting Yanukovych under increasing personal pressure. A week before the planned signing of the deal in November, Yanukovych suddenly reversed his position, discarding it and announcing closer ties with Russia.

This was enough to catalyse growing opposition to his government, and protests began in Kyiv's Independence Square (Maidan Nezalezhnosti). A combination of clumsy heavy-handed police responses and inconsistent messaging from the government only encouraged more to join what became known as the Maidan protests. The government became more desperate, and the largely peaceful protesters were increasingly joined by more

Anti-government militants guard the perimeter of Independence Square, known as the Maidan, in the midst of clashes with the police. (Photo by Brendan Hoffman/ Getty Images)

radical elements. When violence erupted in late January, a protest became a revolution. In February, seeing his power base dwindle, Yanukovych signed an agreement with representatives of the opposition, but when radical protesters stormed government buildings, the Verkhovna Rada, the Ukrainian parliament, voted to impeach him and he fled to Russia. What became known as the Revolution of Dignity – although Yanukovych and the Russian government still describe it as a *coup d'état* – led to the appointment of an interim government under Prime Minister Arseni Yatsenyuk, with elections scheduled for May.

In many ways, the Ukrainian state, especially in the east of the country, went into shock. Local administrations were unsure how to proceed and whom to obey, especially as it was clear that the new government planned to ban officials who had served under Yanukovych from public service.

Vladimir Putin celebrates the seizure of Crimea in August 2014, by which time he had decided also to support and foment rebellion in the Donbas. (Kremlin.ru, CC BY 4.0 https://creativecommons.org/licenses/by/4.0, via Wikimedia Commons)

Meanwhile, a war of words with Moscow would quickly take more serious form when Vladimir Putin seized the moment to take the disputed peninsula of Crimea, with its Russian Black Sea naval bases and predominantly Russophone population.[2] He seems to have had no specific designs on the Donbas at that time, but the spectacle of the almost bloodless seizure of Crimea, followed by a quick (and rigged) referendum and a formal annexation, inspired some elements within the Donbas. That said, at this time, there was still little real popular enthusiasm for independence, let alone their own annexation by Moscow.

However, fears that the new government would be hostile to Russian-speakers, and a desire to use this opportunity to agitate for greater autonomy within Ukraine, led to a series of local protests which, in turn, also sometimes sparked counter-protests by Kyiv loyalists. Moscow expressed its support for the Donbas protesters, but offered nothing but warm words. However, it also did nothing to rein in collections of Russian opportunists, mercenaries and nationalists who began to flock into the Donbas to support the rebels, and their presence radicalized enough of the locals that the conflict deepened. On 12 April, a Russian nationalist commander called Igor Girkin – who went by the callsign 'Strelkov' ('Shooter') – led a ragtag force of volunteers and mercenaries from Crimea across the Russian border into Ukraine, his mobile phone switched off so that no one could order him back. They seized the main police station, the Security Service of Ukraine (SBU) office and a local government building in the town of Sloviansk. Handing out weapons to sympathizers from the government armouries, they quickly took control of the city, and also the nearby Kramatorsk airbase. Kyiv issued a 48-hour ultimatum that came and went, as it desperately tried to muster forces willing and able to respond. The airbase was soon recaptured, but the city of Kramatorsk also fell to anti-Maidan militants. The numbers of rebels were small, but most people – indeed most police, for that matter – even if they did not support the fledgling insurgency, were at least unwilling to fight against it. Meanwhile, as the rebels in Sloviansk managed to hold off successive government assaults, the rebellion spread. Six BMD/BTR-D airborne infantry fighting vehicles (IFVs) and a 2S9 Nona-S self-propelled mortar of the 25th Airmobile Brigade (Bde) either defected to their cause or were appropriated by the insurgents – a furious acting president Olexander Turchinov even toyed with disbanding the brigade in punishment. Momentum, though, seemed to be swinging away from Kyiv.

The Donetsk and Lugansk People's Republics (DNR and LNR, respectively) were declared, as protesters stormed government buildings in not only those, but also other cities in the south and east, sometimes only to be suppressed by local security forces, other times successful. In February, many in the Donbas, while not necessarily happy with Yanukovych, had simply wanted to express their concerns about what the new regime, dominated as they felt it was by Ukrainian-speakers from the west of the country, meant for them. By April, though, a relatively small number of militants, supported, joined and encouraged by Russian nationalists, had hijacked that sentiment to raise the flag of rebellion. In May, the DNR and LNR leaderships would hold referenda on independence from Ukraine. These polls had no legal standing, and were conducted without proper monitoring and often

2 See Raid 59, *Putin Takes Crimea 2014: Grey-zone warfare opens the Russia-Ukraine conflict*

The 'Russian Spring', 2014

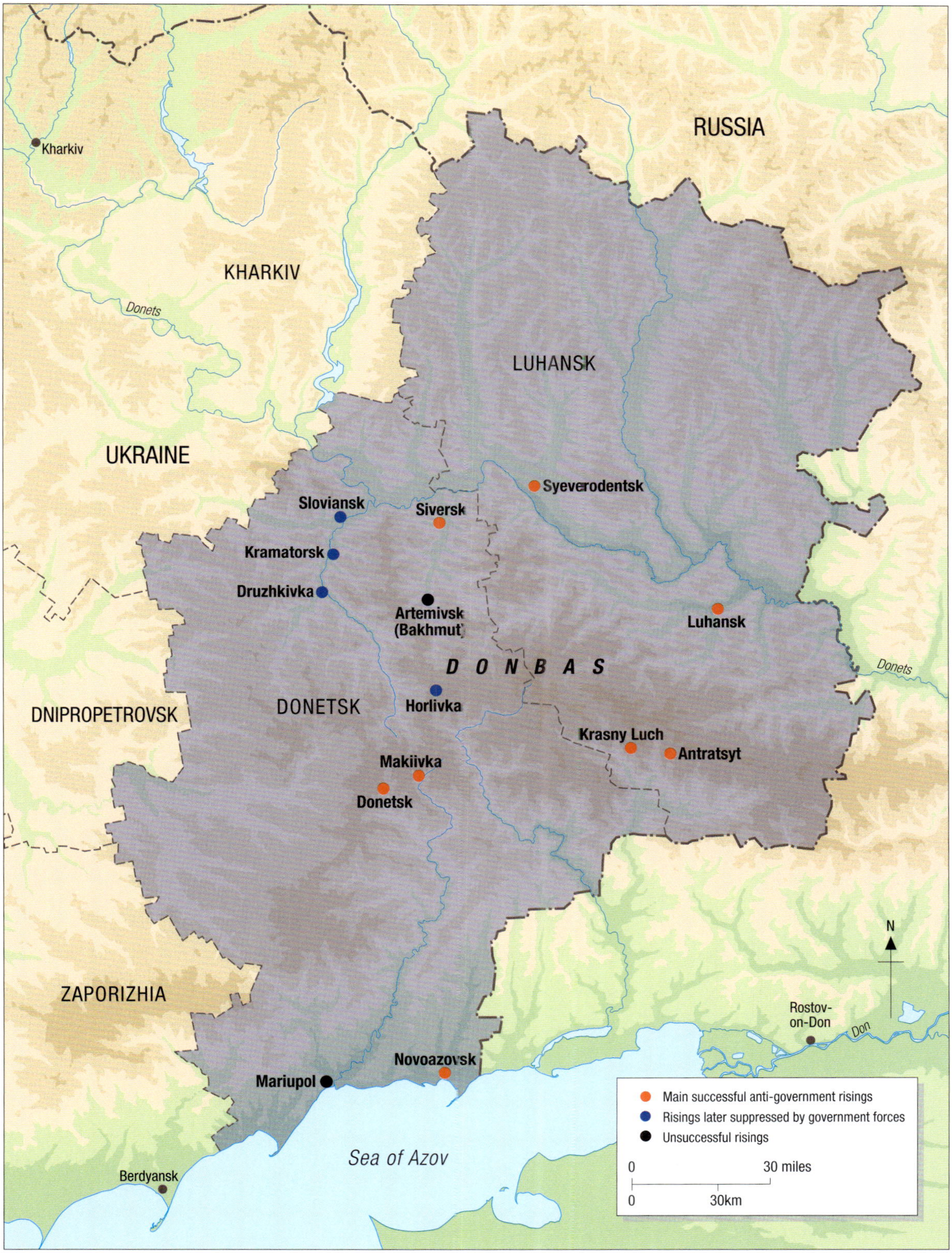

Yanukovych's fall sparked dismay in the Donbas. An anti-Maidan demonstration in Donetsk in May 2014, under a sea of Russian flags. (Andrew Butko, CC BY-SA 3.0 https://creativecommons.org/licenses/by-sa/3.0, via Wikimedia Commons)

under the gun, but nonetheless the rebels duly announced that 89 per cent had voted for independence in the DNR, and 96 per cent in the LNR. On 15 April, Turchinov declared an 'Anti-Terrorist Operation' (ATO), in effect a state of emergency, in the Donbas. This was still a local, largely civil conflict, despite the intervention of outside parties, not yet a war between Russia and Ukraine, but it was the start of the slide to an undeclared war that would eventually lead to the 2022 invasion.

CHRONOLOGY

2013

21 November	Protests begin on Kyiv's Independence Square

2014

18–20 February	Bloody clashes on Independence Square
22 February	Yanukovych flees Kyiv
27 February	Russian 'little green men' (special forces) begin to take Crimea
18 March	Crimea formally annexed by Russia
7 April	Donetsk People's Republic (DNR) declared
12 April	Militants under Igor (Strelkov) Girkin seize Sloviansk
15 April	Acting President Turchinov declares Anti-Terrorist Operation (ATO)
27 April	Lugansk People's Republic (LNR) declared
11 May	Independence referenda in the DNR and LNR
25 May	Petro Poroshenko elected president of Ukraine
26 May	First Battle for Donetsk Airport begins
5 July	Rebel forces retreat from Sloviansk
17 July	Malaysia Airlines Flight MH17 shot down by rebels
10–31 August	Battle of Ilovaisk
23 August	Russian forces cross Ukrainian border
5 September	Minsk Protocol introduces a ceasefire that is quickly broken
19 September	Minsk I peace memorandum signed
29 September	Start of Second Battle for Donetsk Airport

2015

22 January	Donetsk Airport captured by rebels
22 January–18 February	Battle of Debaltseve
12 February	Minsk II agreement
15 February	Minsk II ceasefire formally begins

OPPOSING COMMANDERS

GOVERNMENT

President Petro Poroshenko, elected in May 2014, was both a powerful politician, heading his own party, and also one of the richest men in the country, whose businesses ranged from the Roshen chocolate company to 5 Kanal, the most-watched TV news channel. He had been a prominent supporter of the Revolution of Dignity and campaigned on the rapid suppression of the Donbas rebels, asserting that 'the Anti-Terrorist Operation cannot and should not last two or three months. It should and will last hours.'

Ukraine went through a series of defence ministers in 2014, which did little to help the armed forces weather the early months of the conflict. On 27 February 2014, **Admiral Ihor Tenyukh** replaced the incumbent, **Pavlo Lebedev**, when he, in effect, defected to Crimea during the Russian seizure of the peninsula. With most of the Ukrainian navy essentially captured off Crimea, Tenyukh soon resigned, and on 25 March he was succeeded by **Col. Gen. Mykhailo Koval**. Previously deputy head of the State Border Guard Service (DPSU), Koval lasted in his post until 3 July, before being removed because Poroshenko wanted instead to appoint **Col. Gen. Valery Heletey**. He, too, came not from the military but the security services: he had been a Soviet Border Guard and then a police officer and head of the State Security Administration, the agency protecting government officials. Heletey was more eager than his predecessors, but also presided over a series of setbacks, notably the disaster at Ilovaisk, and also a number of gaffes, such as his groundless claim that Moscow had threatened the use of nuclear weapons. On 12 October, he was dismissed and replaced by **Gen. Stepan Poltorak**. Previously the commander of the National Guard, the body created to incorporate the militias which sprang up during the crisis, Poltorak proved a rather more capable figure and lasted in post all the way to 2019.

President Petro Poroshenko at the unveiling of the monument to Ivan Mazepa, Hetman of the Zaporizhian Cossacks, who switched sides during the Great Northern War between Russia and Sweden. (Oleg Dubyna, CC BY-SA 2.0 https://creativecommons.org/licenses/by-sa/2.0, via Wikimedia Commons)

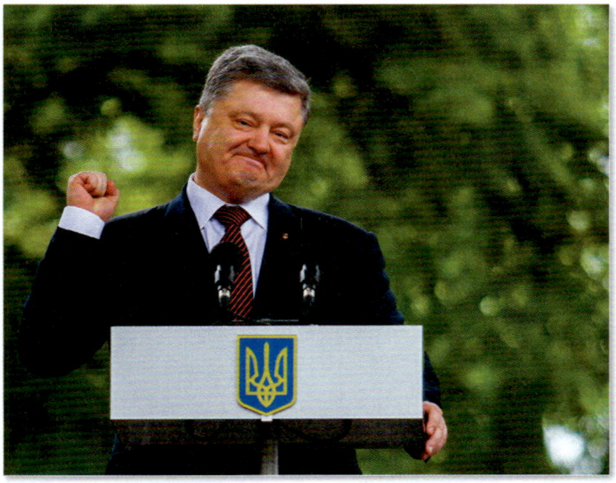

Considering the chaos at the ministry, the role of the Chief of the General Staff – in effect, the overall operational commander of the armed forces – became all the more

Ukrainian soldiers waiting for orders in Ilovaisk, 26 August 2014. Years of systematic neglect had meant that the armed forces were in a poor state by the time of the Donbas conflict. (Роман Зіненко, CC BY-SA 4.0 https://creativecommons.org/licenses/by-sa/4.0, via Wikimedia Commons)

crucial. The pro-Russian **Admiral Yury Ilyin** was dismissed on 28 February, after Yanukovych's flight, and replaced by **Lt. Gen. Mykhailo Kutsyn**, a former tank commander. On 3 July, Poroshenko relieved him of his duties, claiming he was still recovering from shell shock sustained in the Donbas (a claim some have disputed) and appointed his deputy, **Lt. Gen. Viktor Muzhenko**. A well-regarded officer whose time as first deputy commander of the Ukrainian peacekeeping brigade in Iraq meant that Western partners were happy to work with him, and whose decision to leave Yanukovych's Party of Regions before the Revolution of Dignity demonstrated political savvy, Muzhenko would also remain in that position until 2019, when new president Volodymyr Zelensky was looking to put his own stamp on the military hierarchy.

The operational commander was the head of the ATO, **Maj. Gen. Viktor Nazarov**. He would prove a controversial choice, politically well-connected, but in many ways the epitome of an older generation of Soviet-trained officers who mistrusted initiative (which included the maverick attitudes of many of the volunteer battalions) and relied on discipline, formality and bureaucracy. Gen. Muzhenko recounted that, when Donetsk Airport was first attacked by rebels, 'there was no decision, while I was meant to send telegrams to the president, the minister of defence, head of general staff, head of the SBU... and the head of the National Security Council... We sent telegrams to five addresses and awaited a decision. As I understand it, they were deliberating among themselves.' In fairness, Nazarov was trying to fight an insurgency while also creating a new military establishment from scratch, but nonetheless he acquired a reputation for reacting slowly, whether to enemy attacks or to allow his own men to withdraw in untenable circumstances, a tendency that arguably persisted beyond his tenure.

While theatre commanders such as **Lt. Gen. Ruslan Khomchak, Lt. Gen. Petro Lytvyn** and **Maj. Gen. Olexander Syrsky**, who headed the ATO's Sectors B, D and S, respectively, would play crucial roles in this campaign, in many ways it was the men who founded and led the main loyalist militias who were more important, especially in the early days. The

A Ukrainian soldier holds a 7.62mm PKM light machine gun as he stands on top of his BTR-80A armoured personnel carrier (APC) in Al Kut, Iraq, during Operation *Iraqi Freedom* (2003). (LCPL Andrew Williams, USMC, public domain, via Wikimedia Commons)

New recruits for the Azov Battalion (Bn) swear an oath of allegiance near the monument to Bogdan Khmelnitsky in the centre of Kyiv, June 2014. (Photo by Anatolii Stepanov/ Anadolu Agency/Getty Images)

nationalist politician **Dmytro 'Hawk' Yarosh**, for example, was central to the foundation of the Right Sector political movement and its fighting wing, the Ukrainian Volunteer Corps, although in 2015 he left his own party, claiming it had become dominated by figures too interested in 'pseudo-revolutionary activity'. **Andriy Biletsky** had also been one of the founders of Right Sector, but split from it and founded his own movement and military unit, Azov.

DNR

The first head of what became the DNR was the Ukrainian political activist **Pavel Gubarev**, who was acclaimed as 'People's Governor' of the Donetsk region by a gathering of pro-Russian agitators at a meeting in the city's Lenin Square on 1 March 2014. He led the occupation of the Donetsk Regional State Administration building, but a few days later was arrested by the SBU. In May, he was released in a prisoner exchange but by then he had essentially been sidelined by the rise of other political figures, notably the recently elected DNR prime minister, Alexander Borodai. His role became increasingly meaningless, and his efforts to create a new platform for himself, founding the Novorossiya party and planning to stand for election in November, came to nothing. His party was excluded from the elections and Gubarev himself narrowly escaped assassination in October when his car was ambushed.

Alexander Borodai (right), Prime Minister of the Donetsk People's Republic, and the Russian nationalist militant Igor 'Strelkov' Girkin (left) at a press conference in Donetsk, in July 2014. (Photo by Soner Kilinc/ Anadolu Agency/Getty Images)

Instead, power had shifted to the position of prime minister. Initially, this was **Alexander Borodai**, a Russian citizen who had previously been an adviser to Sergei Aksyonov, the gangster-turned-politician whom the Russians appointed as the first head of annexed Crimea. A political operator of nationalist leanings, he was closely associated with the Russian nationalist businessman Konstantin Malofeyev, and his appointment as prime minister came as a surprise to many as he had no real connections to the Donbas. However, he seems to have been installed at the request – demand – of either the Russian government or else certain powerful interest groups within it. Borodai, who stepped down in August 2014, would at one stage boast that he was sent to Donetsk to coordinate 'a special operation of Russian special services'.

Alexander Zakharchenko takes the oath of office as the Prime Minister of the Donetsk People's Republic on 8 August 2014. (newsanna/ANNA-News Official Stream, CC BY 3.0 https://creativecommons.org/licenses/by/3.0, via Wikimedia Commons)

Borodai's successor was the militant commander **Alexander Zakharchenko.** Born in Donetsk, he became head of the local branch of Oplot (Stronghold), a pro-Russian militant movement, which would be at the forefront of the initial rising in Donetsk itself. As a result, he became commander of the city's rebel militia and then its military commandant. In this capacity, he led DNR forces from the front, being wounded in fighting in July (and then again in February 2015) and then being made a major general in the self-proclaimed armed forces of the DNR. His appointment to succeed Borodai in August 2014 appeared to be part of an effort to make the DNR look like a genuinely organic Donetsk phenomenon, and in questionable and internationally disregarded elections held in November 2014, he was confirmed in place with a 79 per cent share of the vote.

The first defence minister of the DNR, **Igor Khakimzyanov**, had a brief and relatively ignominious tenure. Born in Makeyevka, he had trained to be a military pilot until a traffic accident cut his career short. An active participant in the so-called 'Donetsk Anti-Maidan', he was made the DNR's defence minister in April. In May, he was leading an ambush against the pro-Kyiv Azov Bn near Mariupol, when he was captured. Although he was returned in September in a prisoner exchange, he had been replaced in his role by Strelkov and was also in disgrace, so he joined the DNR's Cossack militias and eventually became commander of the 2nd Base of the Cossack Union of the Don Army.

Key militia commanders of the DNR included **Alexander Khodakovsky**, who had defected from the SBU's elite Alpha counter-terrorist commando team and became commander of the Vostok Bn with the codename 'Skif' ('Scythian') and **Igor Bezler**, known by his callsign 'Bes' ('Devil'). A paratrooper, Bezler had fought in the Soviet invasion of Afghanistan and during the Chechen Wars,

Oplot

Oplot (Stronghold) was a political movement founded in Kharkiv in 2010. It had a sports and martial arts wing that generated streetfighters who would often clash with Ukrainian nationalists, and during the Revolution of Dignity became a backbone of the anti-Maidan forces. After an unsuccessful attempt to seize power in Kharkiv, most of its members moved to Donetsk following the militants' successful rising there, and came under the sway of the leader of the Donetsk branch of Oplot, Alexander Zakharchenko. In March, volunteers from the movement formed the basis of the Oplot Bn, which became a brigade in September, including not just three mechanized or motorized regiments but also an armoured company, artillery and AA (anti-air) assets. Formally known as the 5th Separate MR (Motor Rifle) Bde, it would prove both one of the most effective and disciplined units within the DNR's forces, but also a basis of Zakharchenko's power.

DNR forces prepare an artillery attack on Ukrainian positions under the orders of Olga Kachura, who went by the callsign 'Korsa'. A former lieutenant colonel in the Ukrainian police, she joined the DNR's forces during the 'Russian Spring'. She was the only female commander of a DNR artillery unit, and would end up as a colonel in the 3rd Separate MR Bde. (Photo by Pierre Crom/ Getty Images)

and according to the SBU had then worked within the GRU, leaving with the rank of lieutenant colonel. Having been born in Crimea, he returned to Ukraine in 2002. In 2014, he played a role, still unclear, in the seizure of Crimea, then headed to the Donbas, where he led the seizure of a police HQ in Horlivka and became a major general in the DNR's forces. Even by the standards of the rebel militia, he was considered something of a bloody-handed figure, openly calling for the execution of prisoners. In October 2014, he returned to Crimea.

LNR

Valery Bolotov was elected 'People's Governor' of the Lugansk People's Republic in elections in May. He had served as a senior sergeant in the Soviet 103rd Guards Airborne Division (Abn Div) in 1989–90 and in that capacity was deployed to help quell inter-ethnic violence in Georgia and Armenia. In the 1990s, he set himself up in business but quickly took up arms in 2014. He survived an assassination attempt in May, when his car was machine-gunned, and was treated inside Russia. While returning to Luhansk, he was detained by Ukrainian troops, but freed when LNR forces attacked the checkpoint where he was being held. In August 2014, he resigned his position.

His successor was **Igor Plotnitsky**, a former major in the Soviet artillery who would memorably challenge Ukrainian president Poroshenko to a duel to determine the outcome of the war (an offer Poroshenko felt he could refuse). Following the Revolution of Dignity, he established the rebel Zarya (Dawn) Bn and was then appointed the LNR's defence minister, before becoming head of the republic. In the November 2014 elections, he won

Rebels outside the SBU building in Luhansk in April 2014 waving Russian flags and also, on the figure in the foreground, bearing a St George's ribbon, increasingly a symbol of Russian imperial ambition in Ukraine. (Photo by DIMITAR DILKOFF/AFP via Getty Images)

63 per cent of the vote and his Peace for Luhansk Region party gained a majority in the LNR's parliament.

The defence minister of the LNR was originally **Oleg Bugrov**, a former member of the Ukrainian Berkut riot police, who was dismissed in November when he came under suspicion of plotting against Plotnitsky. He left for Russia, where he was arrested in November 2014 and charged with embezzlement. His successor was **Sergei Ignatov**, who lasted until April 2015, when he was replaced by **Yevgeny Morgun**. None of these particularly made his mark, especially because of the relatively weak LNR chain of command. Much more significant were Russian curators such as **Lt. Gen. Ivannikov** and especially forceful militia commanders. **Alexander Mozgovoi**'s Prizrak (Ghost) Bde was arguably the single most effective unit in the LNR, while **Alexander 'Batman' Bednov** commanded arguably the most notorious.

Cossack fighters from Antratsyt, who had rejected Pavel Dryomov's vision of an independent Cossack Republic of Stakhanov. The tricolour flag on the side of the BMP's turret is that of the Don Cossack Host. (Photo by Pierre Crom/ Getty Images)

Dryomov's Cossack Republic

One of the most unusual commanders was the former bricklayer Pavel Dryomov. In September 2014, he declared the micro-state of the Cossack Republic of Stakhanov in the town of Kadiivka (which had formerly been called Stakhanov, after a 'shock worker' of the Stalinist era). Militant in his repudiation of not only Kyiv but also Moscow ('neither Poroshenko nor Putin are interested in an honest country!'), Dryomov was more of a fantasist than a visionary, but he did attract to Kadiivka several hundred Ukrainian and Russian Cossacks committed to his vision. Most Cossacks gravitated towards other units, especially those based in the city of Antratsyt, and as their relationship with Plotnitsky worsened, Dryomov tried to appeal to their concerns by accusing the LNR's leader of embezzlement. This could have contributed to his death the following year, blown up by a car bomb on the day after his wedding.

RUSSIAN

Although **President Vladimir Putin** was clearly the ultimate decision-maker on the Russian side, at this stage of his long-running conflict with Ukraine, he very much avoided being involved directly, in stark contrast to his enthusiasm for the seizure of Crimea. Later, driven by his fundamental view that Ukraine was both an artificial state and one which needed to remain within Moscow's sphere of influence, he would agree first to the provision of substantive military materiel and then the deployment of Russian regulars, but even then, this was on a case-by-case basis and officially – if not especially plausibly – denied.

His main political representative in the Donbas was **Vladislav Surkov**. A publicist and political operator, he was the presidential aide charged with maintaining Russian influence in the post-Soviet region. As such, he would end up exercising considerable influence behind the scenes, until his dismissal in 2020, but in the early stages, arguably a more significant role was played by a series of senior military officers sent in to both support and housetrain the scattered rebel militias. Operating covertly and only using callsigns, they were based in Krasnodon, close to the Russian border, and

After so-called 'vacationers' – volunteers allowed to go and serve with the rebels – in due course Moscow would decide to send its regular troops into Ukraine, like these well-equipped professionals in the latest Ratnik kit. (Photo by The Asahi Shimbun via Getty Images)

also managed the supply of weapons, equipment and volunteers. The most significant was **Col. Gen. Nikolai Tkachyov ('Delfin')**, a former senior military adviser to Syria. Strelkov would later note that while he was 'a good military specialist... all of his military experience is in commanding regular troops, where there's discipline, unconditional obedience. And here, there is partisan warfare, scattered units. He did all that he could, but he was not able to take full command. He was only able to coordinate between separate units.' He would play a particular role in the period known as the 'Northern Wind', when Russian troops were sent directly into the Donbas, but by October 2014, he would be replaced by **Maj. Gen. Sergei Kuzovlev ('Tambov')**, who took over direct command of the DNR's 1st Army Corps in Ukraine until late 2015. Kuzovlev would later become the commander of the Southern Military District's newly formed 8th Guard Combined Arms Army.

Lt. Gen. Oleg Ivannikov ('Orion') was a career military intelligence (GU) officer who, under the pseudonym Andrei Laptev, already had experience working in Russian proxy states, having served the self-proclaimed Republic of South Ossetia as chairman of the Security Council (2004–06) and then Minister of Defence and Emergencies (2006–08). Apparently confirming that there was a de facto division of responsibility, with the GU taking the lead with the LNR and the Federal Security Service (FSB) with the DNR, he was installed as overall 'curator' in Russian parlance, managing not so much the operational military affairs – which was the responsibility of the Krasnodar 'set' – but the LNR's politics. Nonetheless, there was also an FSB representative in Luhansk, **Col. Igor Yegorov ('Elbrus')**, a veteran of its elite Vympel special operations unit. Meanwhile, the army's **Col. Gen. Sergei Istrakov** was given responsibility as military liaison to the DNR, while in July 2014, **Lt. Gen. Vladimir Antyufeyev**, a veteran of other Russian proxy conflicts in Moldova and Georgia working on behalf of the FSB, was installed as the DNR's Minister of State Security.

The greatest impact, though, arguably came from the activities of a Russian FSB officer working without apparent official sanction. **Igor Girkin ('Strelkov')** described himself as the man who 'pulled the trigger' on the Donbas war, and it is probably an accurate assessment. An outspoken Russian nationalist, he was a keen military re-enactor, but no mere wannabe, as he had also been an artillery officer in the Soviet military and would rise to the rank of colonel in the FSB, serving in a special forces role in Chechnya, as well as being either a volunteer or deniable covert asset supporting pro-Moscow separatists in Moldova in 1992, and Serbs in the 1992–95 Bosnian War. He proved a ruthless and competent commander, and was made minister of defence of the DNR in April 2014. However, his uncompromising views and his involvement in the shooting down of the airliner MH17 made him both an embarrassment and a political threat to Moscow. He became increasingly critical of what he saw as Russia's half-hearted support for the Donbas rebellions, and in August he was dismissed from his position under Kremlin pressure. He returned to Russia, where he continued to be a vocal critic of Putin's government, even after his eventual arrest in 2023.

OPPOSING FORCES

GOVERNMENT

It is hard to overstate the degree to which, even before the Revolution of Dignity, the Ukrainian armed forces (ZSU) had been hollowed out. Training had been neglected, procurement delayed (leaving the troops largely equipped with Soviet-era kit) and, although conscription had been abolished, the government failed to offer competitive salaries to attract professionals, so units were calamitously understrength. Then, a combination of desertions by anti-Maidan officers and men and the machinations of Russian agents ensured their functional collapse. Much the same was true of the paramilitary forces of the Interior Ministry (MVS) – although its Berkut (Golden Eagle) riot police were in any case disbanded after the Maidan – and even the SBU's smaller but relatively elite units. Although Kyiv was to reinstate conscription in May 2014 and also carry out two mobilizations of reservists in June, many of those recalled to arms were neither willing nor able to fight.

There were a painfully small number of honourable exceptions. Most of the professional contract servicemen were to be found in five brigades that were more-or-less operational, even if none of them was at anything like its establishment strength. They were often, such as in the case of the so-called 'cyborgs' who defended Donetsk Airport, capable of extraordinary displays of grit, though. Most notional brigades, which would be meant to field three to four battalions plus supporting units, with some 4,000 soldiers in total, were closer to a reinforced battalion in actual strength. There were also some special forces units which were still operational:

- 30th Mech Bde
- 25th Abn Bde
- 79th Airmobile Bde
- 80th Air Assault Bde
- 85th Airmobile Bde
- 3rd Special Forces Rgt
- 4th Special Forces Rgt

Beyond these, there was also a wide range of militarized units subordinated either to the MVS or the Security Service of Ukraine. The Interior Troops, an internal security force within the MVS, was turned into the National Guard which, in turn, became a structure able to absorb some of the volunteer

Well-equipped government troops armed with AK-74 rifles and AKS-74U assault carbines ride a BTR APC during a mission to clear rebel roadblocks outside Sloviansk in April 2014. (Photo by Pierre Crom/ Getty Images)

battalions described below. Some of its elements, like the Liut (Fury) Bde of the Special Patrol Police, recruited specially from serving police officers, would play a particular role in the Donbas campaign. It also included various specialist forces such as the Scorpion and Omega anti-terrorist commando teams. Likewise, the SBU contained within its number several anti-terrorist commando forces, principally the Alpha Group, which would be pressed into service in the Donbas. In March, for example, Alpha operators evacuated Andrei Shishatsky, the loyalist ex-governor of Donetsk, when he was attacked by rebels. Later, they would increasingly find themselves on the front line during some of the most pivotal battles of the campaign.

Over the course of the first year, of course, the ZSU was gradually able to expand its operational units, especially with the reinstatement of conscription and also a mobilization of reservists. While many of these new soldiers were

The government's Mi-24 helicopter gunships would prove vulnerable to rebel and then Russian air defences, but nonetheless were often a crucial source of fire support for beleaguered army units, using both rockets and guns. (Ministry of Defence of Ukraine, CC BY-SA 2.0 https://creativecommons.org/licenses/by-sa/2.0, via Wikimedia Commons)

THE SECOND BATTLE FOR DONETSK AIRPORT, NOVEMBER 2014 (PP.26–27)

The 'cyborgs' who defended Donetsk Airport with such determination during the second battle, from September 2014 to January 2015, did so under the toughest conditions. Here a collection of Ukrainian soldiers regroup during a sortie into the ruins of the old terminal building on a cold and cheerless day at the start of November. A sniper from the 95th Airmobile Bde **(1)** kneels atop the burnt-out shell of a BMP-1 IFV from the DNR's Oplot Bn, left from earlier fighting, scanning the surroundings through the scope of his SVD rifle. He is being joined by one of the handful of operators from the 73rd Naval Special Operations Centre **(2)** who helped relieve the defenders, in newer pattern digital camouflage and with the 73rd's seahorse unit patch. A soldier from the 93rd Mechanized (Mech) Bde **(3)**, who has just fired his RPG-7 anti-tank launcher, calls to a colleague to hand him a new PG-7VL grenade, while in the background two more soldiers **(4)** lug a 12.7mm NSV Utyos heavy machine gun into cover. Like the other men, the RPG (rocket-propelled grenade) gunner wears the yellow recognition tapes on his sleeves worn by some Ukrainian troops to ensure they were not confused with rebel fighters who were often wearing the same or similar uniforms.

sent to these existing units to fill gaps in the strength or make up for losses, others were used to bring new ones to a usable status, such as the 51st Separate Mech Bde and the 17th Tank Bde.

The air force was in an arguably even more parlous state. It had 144 airframes on its books in 2014, but at least a third were simply not in flying condition, and many of the rest suffered from years of inadequate maintenance. Pilots likewise rarely had the amount of real flying experience needed to keep their skills up to scratch. In one tactical aviation brigade, for example, half the pilots had flown only on simulators throughout 2013. Nonetheless, they flew in the campaign, and often well – or at least with daring. As well as transport aircraft, Mi-24 helicopter gunships, Mi-8 assault and transport helicopters and Su-25 ground attack aircraft were especially evident, especially in the earlier months, although this became less viable as the militias began to be supplemented by Russian regulars with their more advanced AA systems, who also sometimes operated under the cover of air superiority fighters flying from bases over the border.

Ukraine's small navy was largely lost to destruction, capture or defection during the Crimean annexation. Similarly, most of its Naval Infantry Corps had been on Crimea, and so it went into the Donbas campaign only with a small remnant of the 36th Separate Coastal Defence Bde composed of 200 marines of its 1st Bn, who had managed to leave Crimea under Lt. Col. Dmytro Delyatytsky. The only fully operational element was the 73rd Naval Special Operations Centre, which would see action at Donetsk Airport and Debaltseve.

THE VOLUNTEER BATTALIONS

When Russian-backed insurgencies began sprouting in the south and east, they were countered by a motley array of 'volunteer battalions' – rarely, if ever, anywhere near battalion-strength – recruited from ordinary locals,

A woman drops money into a collection box for donations to the Azov Bn, which like so many of the volunteer units had to raise shortfalls in operational funds through donations, whether from political movements, oligarchs or ordinary people in the street. Note the controversial symbol on the soldier's patch, which many consider akin to the *Wolfsangel* used on the badge of the 2nd SS Panzer Division in World War II. (Photo by Sean Gallup/Getty Images)

Donbas Bn recruits in training: note the variety of uniforms and weapons, typical of the volunteer units, especially at this time. (Photo by Andrew Burton/Getty Images)

opportunist mercenaries, political activists and any other constituency willing to fight to hold their country together. Some were essentially the pet projects of oligarchs who either supported the new order or who saw a political threat in potential secession, such as Ihor Kolomoisky (who had been appointed governor of Dnipropetrovsk and bankrolled a number of such units) or the coal baron turned financier Renat Akhmetov, who did not raise specific units but gave huge amounts of money. Others were really local self-defence forces, generated when they saw a danger to their region or city. Kharkiv-1 and Kharkiv-2, for example, were called special police battalions, but were at first actually just hastily sworn-in locals. The most controversial would be those springing from political movements, usually (though not exclusively) nationalists and far-rightists, such as Azov and Right Sector. Many had to turn to fundraising at home and abroad to buy even the basics. Nonetheless, by August 2014, the official figure was that in total these units comprised some 4,000 fighters, while many estimates on the ground suggest it could have been as many as twice that.

They were quickly formally brought into the ZSU or else the forces of the MVS, in order to give them a certain legal standing, but through 2014–15, this was often no more than the thinnest of pretences, and some political units such as Right Sector and the OUN (Organization of Ukrainian Nationalists) would not accept such subordination. In any case, many of these militias had no intention of obeying a formal command structure they regarded as hidebound, conservative and quite possibly of questionable loyalty. At the same time, Kyiv was often unwilling or unable to pay or equip them properly, further weakening the chain of command. That did not by any means indicate that coordination was poor: many units liaised with each other directly and effectively, and some officers, such as Col. Yuri Sodol, commander of the 25th Abn Bde, acquired the reputation of being able to work well with the volunteer battalions. At other times, though, mutual incomprehension and jealousies, as well as practical issues such as a lack of common doctrines and communications protocols, would prove problematic.

Even though most were effectively confined to their home regions during this campaign, many of the ZSU's motorized infantry territorial defence battalions (TDBs) were originally volunteer battalions. The 34th TDB, for example, was raised in Kirovohrad and funded by the Batkivshchyna party of former prime minister Yulia Timoshenko. The TDBs included:

- 3rd Lviv TDB
- 6th Ternopil TDB
- 9th Vinnytsia TDB
- 10th Zhytomyr TDB
- 13th Chernihiv TDB
- 15th Sumy TDB
- 19th Mykolaiv TDB

Soldiers of the Sich Special Patrol Police Bn parading under the flag of the nationalist Svoboda party. Their unit patch shows a stylized Cossack head. (Pryshutova Viktoria, CC BY 3.0 https://creativecommons.org/licenses/by/3.0, via Wikimedia Commons)

- 21st Kherson TDB
- 22nd Kharkiv TDB
- 24th 'Aidar' TDB (Luhansk)
- 34th 'Batkivshchyna' TDB (Kirovohrad)
- 37th Zaporizhia TDB
- 40th 'Kryvbas' TDB (Dnipropetrovsk)
- 41st Chernihiv TDB

At this time, the main volunteer battalions subordinated to the MVS via the police or National Guard (many of which again had a political dimension – the Sich Bn, for example, was recruited largely from members of the far-right Svoboda party) were:

- 1st 'Kulchitsky' Bn
- Azov Bn
- Dnipro-1 Bn
- Dnipro-2 Bn
- Donbas Bn
- Kharkiv Police Bn
- Myrotvorets Bn (Kyiv)
- Poltava Bn
- Shakhtarsk Bn (Dnipropetrovsk)
- Sich Bn (Kyiv)
- Svyatyi Mykolai Bn (Mykolaiv)

Azov

One of the most controversial of the volunteer battalions, the Azov Bn was founded by radical nationalist Andriy Biletsky in Mariupol in May, officially taking its name from the Azov Sea, but arguably more of its inspiration from the iconography of the far right. It was eventually incorporated into the National Guard in November, being formally re-designated the Azov Special Operations Detachment or the Azov Regiment (Rgt), later becoming a full brigade. While questions were sometimes raised about its obedience to the chain of command, it acquired a reputation as a hard-fighting unit, which would see action in both Ilovaisk and the Second Battle for Donetsk Airport.

The government forces were not the only ones to have Chechens on their side. Chechens like this fighter also fought for the rebels, sometimes as volunteers, sometimes mercenaries and sometimes deniable contingents sent by Moscow. (Photo by Pierre Crom/ Getty Images)

Finally, there were also some units which refused to subordinate themselves to Kyiv, even notionally, or else which otherwise fell between the organizational cracks for political reasons. They included two 'battalions' (both closer to company strength) of Chechen émigrés opposed to both Moscow and its proxy regime in Chechnya, another raised by the OUN and, largest of all, the Ukrainian Volunteer Corps raised by Right Sector, that at its peak claimed to number 5,000 men (other accounts put it closer to 2,500) in three motorized battalions.

- Dzhokar Dudayev Bn (Chechen)
- Georgian National Legion (Georgian)
- OUN Bn
- Right Sector Ukrainian Volunteer Corps
- Sheikh Mansur Bn (Chechen)

DNR

The Donetsk People's Militia was formally established by Pavel Gubarev in March 2014, but at the time was not a real structure; there was no common chain of command, and any coordination was ad hoc, through the direct negotiations of unit leaders. It was little more than an umbrella title for various local gangs and units, often cohering around charismatic leaders or

Why 'militias'?

The Russian word *opolcheniye*, which is best translated as militias, carries with it a powerful historical charge. In medieval accounts, it was sometimes used to denote a mass, popular mobilization against an enemy. However, the term is most directly associated with the First and Second People's Militia, which drove Polish–Lithuanian occupiers out of Moscow in 1611–12. Later, similar national mobilizations took place in the Napoleonic and Crimean wars and in World War II, but the classic image of the *opolchentsy* (militiamen) was defined by the liberation of Moscow in 1612. The use of the term by the DNR and LNR was clearly intended to give their collections of thugs and nationalists a degree of legitimacy both at home and with the Russian public.

A ragtag collection of militias at a barricade in Sloviansk. Note the DNR flag and the array of recognition tapes on sleeves which, being of so many different colours, somewhat misses the point. (Photo by GENYA SAVILOV/AFP via Getty Images)

political movements. Strelkov, after assuming notional overall control, tried to establish a more meaningful command structure, especially once Moscow began involving itself more directly, as it meant he had leverage over the individual commanders, essentially being able to influence their access to the vital supplies, weapons and ammunition being brought over the border. However, as he was at the same time still involved in field command, his ability to do much before he was dismissed in August 2014 was limited.

Although, over time, efforts were made to at least pretend that the heterogeneous militias were part of a regularized military, with the formal establishment of the 1st Army Corps on 12 November 2014, this remained an essentially cosmetic process until after 2015. Units had their own organizations, uniforms, ways of fighting, recruitment feeds and, often, territories – the dividing line between some of these militias and organized crime groups, street gangs or warlords' retinues was often hazy – while commanders were frequently wilful, to the degree that in due course Moscow would begin a campaign of selective assassination to eliminate the most troublesome and bring the rest to heel.

A partial order of battle of the 1st Army Corps on its formation was:

- Donetsk Republican Guard
- 1st Separate MR Bde (formerly Sloviansk Bde)
- Kalmius Bde
- Oplot Bde
- Vostok Bde
- 15th International Bde
- Mariupol-Khingan Rgt
- Miners' Bn
- Somalia Bn
- Sparta Bn
- Voskhod Bn
- Russian Orthodox Army

A rebel volunteer wearing a helmet with a sticker of the self-declared Donetsk People's Republic watches as government forces arrive in an Mi-8 helicopter to take position on the outskirts of Sloviansk on 2 May 2014. (Photo by Pierre Crom/Getty Images)

Many of these units were nowhere near the strength that their title would suggest. The Republican Guard, for example, was treated as a brigade-strength force with an eventual establishment of 3,000 men in six battalions, but in practice it was rarely at more than half that. They also often proved ephemeral. The Steppe Bn, which numbered a couple of companies of Cossacks at most, appeared in June 2014 and had disbanded by the end of July, individual fighters drifting into other units or heading home. The Russian Orthodox Army – really an understrength battalion – would be absorbed into Oplot in late 2014. Many others were so closely linked with their founders and commanders that they were virtual private armies. Sometimes, they would outlast them. The Somalia Bn, for example, was founded by Lt. Col. Mikhail 'Givi' Tolstykh, who chose the name because its fighters were 'as brave as Somalis'. When issued with T-64 and T-72 tanks, it became the 1st Separate 'Somalia' Tank Bn, but after Tolstykh's assassination in 2017, it became the Separate Guards Assault 'Somalia' Bn named after M. S. Tolstykh. In other cases, though, it turned out that the leader was the driving force holding them together. Strelkov's Sloviansk Bde (sometimes known as the 1st Slavic Bde) only just about managed to survive his departure, becoming the 1st Separate MR Bde.

Other units would be added to the 1st Army Corps over time. As the DNR started to be issued more tanks from Russian stockpiles in 2015, primarily T-72B1 models, the Diesel Bn was established to field them, eventually becoming the 1st Corps' 2nd Separate Tank Bn. Similarly, as more artillery began to be provided, the Kalmius Bn, originally a tough motorized infantry unit recruited especially from Donbas miners, became an artillery formation. While Russian volunteers tended to join regular militia units, those from farther afield usually ended up in the 15th International Bde, which was really an umbrella structure for a wide range of national detachments called 'battalions' but in practice anything in size from a platoon to a company (such as the Serbian Jovan Šević Detachment, which had disbanded by the end of 2014).

The Sparta Battalion

Arsen 'Motorola' Pavlov was a Russian national who fought in Strelkov's defence of Sloviansk, heading a machine gun platoon. In August 2014, he established his own unit, which would see its first major engagements in the fighting for Donetsk Airport that autumn. It would then be deployed to the Debaltseve offensive before later moving to Shyrokyne, east of Mariupol. Sparta was a light battalion in every sense, being built around two reconnaissance companies and the Lavina (Avalanche) 'special forces' – assault – company. It was a sign of Pavlov's rather confused nationalist ideology that its symbols mixed the old imperial Russian colours of black, yellow and white, a jagged M derived from a mutant-fighting order in the science-fiction novel *Metro 2033* and a wolf. Pavlov died in October 2016, killed by an improvised explosive in his apartment building, in what has variously been described as a falling-out between criminals or a Kremlin-authorized hit of an overly independent commander.

Although something of an inconvenience to the Kremlin, after his assassination in 2016, Sparta Bn commander Arsen 'Motorola' Pavlov became something of an icon of Donbas resistance. Here a mural dedicated to him in St Petersburg claims that 'there is no death' for him. (Vadim Tolbatov, CC BY-SA 4.0 https://creativecommons.org/licenses/by-sa/4.0, via Wikimedia Commons)

The Kalmius Battalion

The Kalmius Bn (named after a river in the region) was established by Valentin Motuzenko ('Ataman Ivanych') in Donetsk in June 2014, drawn especially from local miners, hence its nickname of the 'miners' battalion'. Its original strength was around 500 and, by July–August, it was one of the DNR's main assault units, taking part in battles at Snizhne, Torez and Shakhtarsk. At the end of August, as Russian equipment started to arrive in greater numbers, it was reorganized as an artillery brigade equipped with 122mm 2S1 self-propelled guns (SPGs) and D-30 howitzers, and also a regiment of BM-21 Grad Multiple-Launch Rocket Systems (MLRSs). In this role, it played a significant part at Debaltseve, receiving the World War II-style honorific of 'Guards'. In 2023, it would be incorporated into the Russian armed forces as the 14th Separate 'Kalmius' Artillery Bde.

LNR

The LNR's forces – initially known as the Army of the South-East, then the People's Militia of the LNR, then from October 2014 the 2nd Army Corps – were, if anything, even less coherent and disciplined than those of the DNR. Especially in the formative period of the People's Militia, there was considerable cooperation and interpenetration between them and their Donetsk counterparts. For example, what became the 7th 'Chistyakovskaya' MR Bde was drawn in part from Strelkov's original Sloviansk Bde in 2015, and at one point there was even a question of whether the Prizrak Bde, the single largest and most effective unit in the LNR at this time, was actually going to subordinate itself to Strelkov's command.

A partial order of battle of the 2nd Army Corps on its formation was:

- Prizrak Bde
- Odessa Separate Mech Special Purpose Bde
- 2nd Separate Don Bde
- 4th Separate MR Bde
- 6th Separate 'Matvei Platov' Cossack Rgt
- Separate Commandant's Rgt
- 1st Liberation Bn named after the Holy Blessed Prince Alexander Nevsky
- 3rd Stanichno-Lugansk Abn Bn
- Leshy Bn

Workmen from the DNR's Separate Repair and Refurbishment Bn work on captured government armour, often damaged vehicles seized in battle, which was frequently their main source of such vehicles before Moscow's decision to provide direct assistance. (Photo by Pierre Crom/Getty Images)

- Rus Women's Bn
- USSR Bn
- Zarya People's Liberation Bn
- Separate Recon Bn
- Batman Rapid Response Group
- Cossack National Guard

As should be clear from this catalogue, the 2nd Corps was an array of idiosyncratic and often unmanageable units, usually cohering around a particular region, leader or ideology, few ever reaching their notional establishment strength. The 3rd Stanichno-Lugansk Abn (sometimes called Assault) Bn was a unit drawn largely from former paratroopers who had served in the Soviet war in Afghanistan, for example. Meanwhile, Dmitry 'Lyuti' Pindurin's USSR Bn, despite its nostalgic name, was essentially a local militia from the town of Bryanka, west of Luhansk, which in due course would simply become a territorial defence force. As for the Rus Women's Bn, which was never larger than a company in size, this was originally a companion to the Rus Bn, a unit formed by several hundred workers and security guards from the Krasnodonuglya mine complex. When that was rolled into the 4th Bde, resistance to having a women's unit in the ranks

Prizrak Brigade

It was a mark of the relative weakness of the LNR chain of command that the founder of what was initially the Prizrak (Ghost) Bn, Alexander Mozgovoi, considered himself allied, rather than subordinated, to the political leadership in Luhansk, and was closer to Strelkov until his departure. Prizrak acquired a formidable reputation, and this helped ensure a steady stream of recruits, including Cossacks from both Ukraine and Russia and foreigners from farther afield, most of whom were assigned to its largely Francophone Continental Unit, and into Unit 404, a detachment of foreign communist fighters also known as the Biryukov-Markov Unit. By autumn 2014, it numbered more than 1,600 fighters, and was re-designated as a brigade. Like so many other commanders who failed to appreciate the changing political environment and that they were now expected to be obedient Russian proxies, Mozgovoi was assassinated in May 2015. The unit survived his death, though, becoming the LNR's 4th Separate MR Bde in 2016.

Soldiers from the Cossack National Guard, an LNR unit, sitting atop a tank likely provided by the Russians, during the fighting around Debaltseve in February 2015. The black-yellow-white flag is an old tsarist one, still flown by Russian nationalists. (Photo by Pierre Crom/Getty Images)

meant that it remained separate, withering and disappearing by the end of 2015. Individual female soldiers increasingly became apparent within other units.

The unruly Batman Rapid Reaction Group was disbanded in January 2015 after the assassination of its commander, Alexander 'Batman' Bednov, but even for less bloody reasons, the next few years would see continued rationalization. The infamous Hooligan Bn had already become part of the 2nd Bde along with the Zarya (Dawn) Bn, while the 1st 'Alexander Nevsky' Liberation Bn would soon become incorporated into the Prizrak Bde. On the other hand, 2015 would see the formation of the 1st 'August' Separate Tank Bn under Alexander Kostin, in many ways the LNR's counterpart to the Diesel Bn, the recipient of T-72B tanks from Russia, to supplement the relatively few T-64s (including some of the Ukrainian-variant T-64 Bulats) captured from Kyiv's arsenals or brought over by defectors.

Even more than the DNR, the LNR drew on Cossacks from both Ukraine and Russia for its forces. Many other units recruited from among them, such as Alexei Pavlov's Leshy (Forest Spirit) Bn. The Cossack culture had been all but eradicated in Soviet times, but experienced a massive resurgence in the 1980s and 1990s. Although again subject to periodic mergers and

The Batman Rapid Reaction Group

Its comical name notwithstanding – drawn as it was from the callsign of its founder, former riot policeman Alexander Bednov – this unit became notorious even by the standards of the LNR militia for looting, organized criminality and human rights abuses. It grew to a strength of around 400, incorporating such mixed elements as the so-called Kornilovtsy and the Rusich Sabotage and Assault Recon Group (Russian imperialists and neo-fascists, respectively). In summer 2014, Bednov repudiated the LNR leadership but continued to wage a private war. When threatened with investigation and arrest, though, he brought his unit back into the fold (the militants of Rusich separated from the group, denouncing Bednov's 'cowardice'). However, Bednov's political ambitions, brutal methods and criminal enterprises made him too much of a liability for Moscow, who wanted its militia commanders to know their place. In January 2015, his convoy was ambushed and he was killed, in what is generally assumed to have been a GU operation, and his unit was cannibalized by other elements of the 2nd Corps.

splits, the LNR's Cossack fighters were largely collected into the Cossack National Guard, a unit based at Antratsyt, although at times units such as the Great Host of the Don Cossacks and the 1st Cossack Rgt did emerge from under its shadow. The Cossack National Guard was around 4,000 strong at its peak.

RUSSIAN

In 2014, Russian military doctrine for intervention operations was structured around the use of battalion tactical groups (BTGs), combined-arms manoeuvre units drawn from parent brigades on a mission-specific basis. Given that the Russian military comprises both conscripts (who are barred by law from being deployed outside Russia, except in a time of openly declared war) and *kontraktnik* professionals, BTGs would be drawn solely from the latter and a disproportionate share of the brigade's support elements. A typical BTG might be made up of two to four mechanized companies, a tank company and additional support elements, to a strength of 600–800 soldiers. This would prove an effective instrument in the kind of smaller-scale, shorter-duration and firepower-forward operations the Russians staged in the Donbas, but much less so in the later full-scale invasion of Ukraine. BTGs lacked staying power, the capacity to absorb losses and hold ground in that scale of war. In the 2014–15 Donbas campaign, though, they would be able to deliver powerful strikes when needed to turn the tide of battle when government forces looked as if they would be able to defeat the insurgents.

A (potentially incomplete) list of the units which generated BTGs in the period from April 2014 to March 2015 is:

- 8th Guards MR Bde
- 18th MR Bde
- 20th Separate MR Bde
- 21st Separate MR Bde
- 28th Separate MR Bde
- 32nd Separate MR Bde
- 138th Separate MR Bde

Russian paratroopers (note the folding-stock AKS-74 rifles) in Rostov-on-Don in 2014, the city that would later become the hub for military operations inside the Donbas. (© Vyacheslav Argenberg/ http://www.vascoplanet.com/, CC BY 4.0 https://creativecommons.org/licenses/by/4.0, via Wikimedia Commons)

- 200th Separate MR Bde
- 6th Tank Bde
- 31st Guards Air Assault Bde

In addition, other units deployed fully or in part included the 137th Abn Rgt, 247th Abn Assault Rgt and 331st Abn Rgt, as well as specialists such as engineers and AA missile crews, and also a range of special forces. These included the 2nd, 3rd, 10th and 25th Spetsnaz (Special Designation) Bdes and the Airborne Troops' own 45th Separate Guards Spetsnaz Rgt. Very small numbers of operators from the special forces of the FSB, notably Russia's own Alpha Group, provided security for some personnel deployed to advisory missions in Donetsk and Luhansk. Claims that some also fought at Debaltseve remain unproved and are probably just myths. The Russian Navy, having been so significant in the seizure of Crimea, played no real part in the Donbas campaign. The Aerospace Forces played a growing role in supporting ground attacks and, equally important, posing a sufficient threat to Ukrainian aircraft that they rarely flew missions once Moscow had shown its hand and begun openly operating in the Donbas.

The Spetsnaz of the 45th Rgt were among the forces Moscow deployed to the Donbas, not least as they were elite troops also provided with special equipment, such as this RDA-1 VDV buggy mounting a NSVT heavy machine gun. (Photo by Sasha Mordovets/Getty Images)

OPPOSING PLANS

GOVERNMENT

Initially, it was hard to discern any actual plan on Kyiv's part, not least as the new interim government was still constituting itself and grappling with a military and security apparatus chain of command that had all but broken. Rhetoric about restoring order notwithstanding, little was evident beyond a hope that local security forces – garrisons, police, SBU – would be able to suppress any attempted insurrections on their patches, and then assist neighbouring regions which might be facing greater trouble. A retired Ukrainian SBU official disparagingly described this as 'a strategy of firefighting by crossing one's fingers'.

The irony is that this in many ways freed up the various actors in the Donbas – political radicals, oligarchs, mayors and governors, local security chiefs, army officers – behind the volunteer battalions and other local initiatives, which arguably were more effective at the time than any central government action would have been. Through the spring, not only did these counter-revolutionary forces emerge, but cooperation, intelligence sharing and even practical assistance began to tie many of them together. Still, though, it is not possible to talk of any meaningful strategy beyond resistance.

Over time, however, Kyiv would begin to rise to the challenge. With the declaration of the ATO in June, it increasingly tried to control the struggle

The ZSU was not only hampered by years of neglect, it also had a greater need than the rebels to spare civilians and, indeed, provide them with aid, as seen here following the relief of Sloviansk. (Photo by Soner Kilinc/Anadolu Agency/ Getty Images)

against the rebels and their Russian backers. Often this was a controversial process. Many militia commanders had enjoyed their old autonomy and did not want to become links in a larger chain of command, and there was widespread suspicion about a military high command widely considered to be unimaginative, bureaucratic and, in short, much too 'Soviet'. Nonetheless, as discussed above, through appeals to their patriotic duty, offers of support and sometimes none-too-subtle threats, Kyiv was able to bring most of the volunteers to heel. This allowed the formulation of actual plans, although they tended to be operational more than strategic.

DNR/LNR

The rebel pseudo-states had even less scope to operate in any strategic manner. They were formed through an agglomeration of local insurgencies, and their leaderships emerged through the horse-trading of local militia commanders and strongmen. Their goals were often contradictory, and changed over time, with some wanting to join Russia from the outset, but most simply seeking guarantees and greater autonomy from Kyiv. They soon began pushing Moscow for greater support and open recognition, but while this meant they inevitably had to consider what the Kremlin wanted, they often ignored or simply misunderstood the suggestions and advice they were being given. Indeed, the journalist Anna Arutunyan was able to witness first-hand a meeting of the DNR's ruling junta in which they managed to persuade themselves that Putin's unambiguous warning that they ought *not* to hold a referendum on seceding from Ukraine was actually a coded message that they *should*!

As Russian influence and assistance became more significant, they increasingly came under Moscow's direct sway. Individual leaders and commanders would often have and prosecute their own personal plans, typically as to how to eliminate their rivals and acquire more assets, but it

As the rebel pseudo-states became more organized – and as it became clear that the conflict would be a long one – they had to move beyond relying on volunteers. These are DNR military IDs, issued on 10 February 2015, the first official mobilization day intended to raise an army of 100,000 troops. (Photo by Pierre Crom/Getty Images)

Changing front lines, June 2014–February 2015

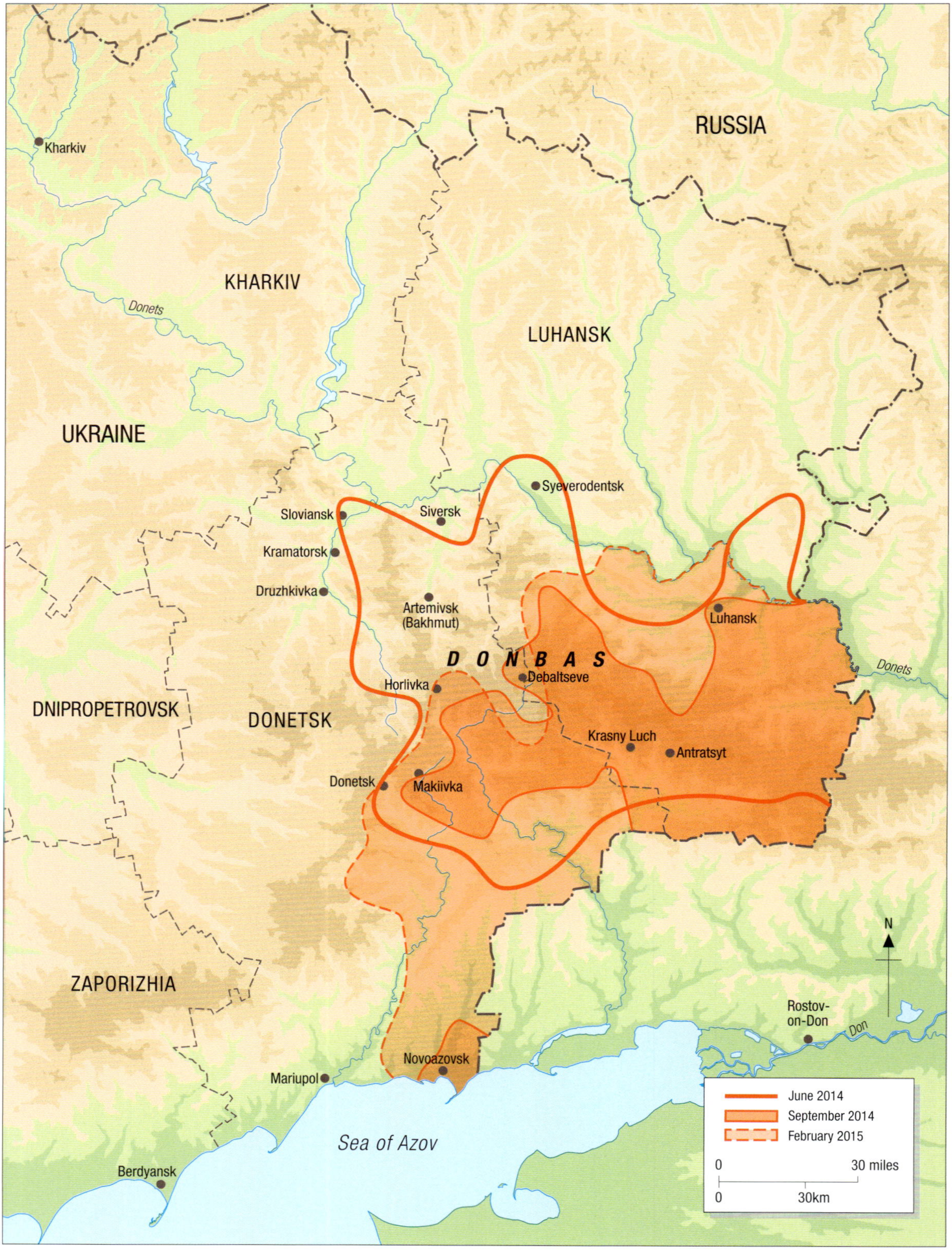

became meaningless to talk about either the DNR or LNR having the agency required to make strategy. As a disillusioned Russian officer assigned as an 'adviser' to the LNR's forces in autumn 2014 put it, 'we gave the orders. The only real question was whether they understood them.'

RUSSIAN

Moscow had originally had no specific plans or even clearly articulated ambitions in the Donbas. Its focus had been on the seizure and annexation of Crimea, and when this sparked insurrection in the Donbas, Putin seems simply to have been willing to maintain a watching brief. There were those eager to encourage the risings, ranging from semi-independent businesspeople like Konstantin Malofeyev, who had once been Strelkov's patron, to officials like Sergei Glaziev, a hawkish economist who was also a presidential aide. Glaziev, for example, was spending his own money in support of the various uprisings. Instead, the official position was neither to hinder nor help on any scale, but rather to see what happened.

A sense would grow in government circles that this rising could not be allowed to fail. In part, this was to avoid a backlash from nationalists at home, but mainly because it seemed it was a useful means of undermining the new regime in Kyiv. There was no enthusiasm for annexing the DNR and LNR, though. The notion was, rather, that Ukraine would be forced to become a more loosely federated republic, with the Donbas reincorporated as Moscow's proxies with a veto on any move towards the West. In due course, Putin would decide that he had to deploy his military to ensure that Kyiv could not simply reconquer the Donbas, but until 2022 he was never especially committed to the rebels, who were no more than a means to a wider end. Russia's interventions were therefore intended to prevent the rebels from being defeated not – much to their frustration – to help them expand their pseudo-states.

Putin (centre) and Defence Minister Sergei Shoigu (left) watching military exercises in 2014. (Photo by MIKHAIL KLIMENTYEV/RIA-NOVOSTI/AFP via Getty Images)

THE CAMPAIGN

THE BATTLES FOR SLOVIANSK AND KRAMATORSK

Strelkov's handful of men, with whom he had taken Sloviansk on 12 April, were soon reinforced by sympathizers from across the Donbas, as Mayor Nelya Shtepa endorsed their seizure of the town. It took time to distribute weapons and form some rough-and-ready rebel administration, though, so it was just as well for them that the initial government response was limited, sporadic and small scale. Meanwhile, anti-Maidan agitators in the neighbouring city of Kramatorsk also struck, taking the city and its airfield. At first, it was unclear whether their risings would spread or be successfully contained. SBU and MVS special forces had quickly arrived on the scene. On 15 April, the Omega Group anti-terrorist unit stormed Kramatorsk airfield and routed a substantially larger number of armed but disorganized militants. A team from the Alpha Group then recaptured a TV tower on nearby Mount Karachun, which had begun transmitting Russian programmes. A couple of platoons of paratroopers from the 25th Bde then drove militants out of the outlying village of Sergeyevka.

These initial response forces, however, could not safely try to storm cities in which the rebels had managed to entrench themselves and where they could count on at least part of the population's active support. Only on 24 April, 12 days after the city was taken, were the first real efforts made against Sloviansk, under Lt. Gen. Vasily Krutov, the newly appointed First Deputy Head of the SBU, who had been shouted down by a crowd of locals when he tried to address them earlier. Even so, this ended up being more about containment and reconnaissance than a full-scale assault. Alpha Group operators swept away several rebel checkpoints on the outskirts and then began to enter the city. They were, however, met with fire, and militants from

The SBU's Lt. Gen. Vasily Krutov appears to have misjudged local feeling and as a result was jostled and shouted at by a pro-rebel crowd outside the Kramatorsk military airbase on 15 April 2014. (Photo by Pierre Crom/Getty Images)

nearby Krasny Lyman rushed to reinforce the defenders. By the middle of the day, the government forces had retreated. Although the plan was to resume the attack the next day, Putin warned Kyiv against the use of force 'against civilians', and Russian troops began manoeuvres within view of Ukrainian border posts. Fearing an escalation, the government commanders suspended the operation, even as rebels launched a diversionary attack on Kramatorsk airfield, destroying an An-2 transport and an Mi-8 helicopter on the ground, while the rest of that adjacent city remained in the hands of anti-government forces.

Kyiv opted instead to try and blockade Sloviansk, to starve it of reinforcements and resupply, while launching small-scale attacks against rebel checkpoints around the city, slowly to close the noose. Government forces were able to push the rebels closer to the centre of Sloviansk, but not without losses, including two Mi-24 gunships shot down by 9K310 Igla-1 (SA-16) or 9K38 Igla (SA-18) MANPADS seized from Ukrainian arsenals. An Mi-8 assault helicopter was also damaged by small arms fire. By this stage, the size of the insurgent force in Sloviansk was estimated as anything up to 800 effectives. Meanwhile, new units were joining the siege, largely volunteer battalions hastily enrolled into the National Guard, such as the 1st 'Kulchitsky' Bn, made up of militants who had helped defend the Maidan during the Revolution of Dignity, and which went on to fight at both Sloviansk and Kramatorsk.

After an ultimatum demanding the rebels lay down their arms and surrender was rejected, on the night of 3 May, the attack resumed. A column of troops from the 95th Airmobile Bde in trucks and armoured fighting vehicles (AFVs) tried to force their way through Yasnohirka, a village between Sloviansk and Kramatorsk. The goal was to prevent militants in the respective cities from supporting each other, but they were delayed long enough by a crowd of locals supportive of the insurgents for armed rebels to set up a defence. Nonetheless, the paratroopers were ultimately able to prevail, while a mix of regulars and volunteer battalion forces including the National Guard's 16th Public Order Protection Bde made an assault on Kramatorsk that retook all but the centre of the city. Just as the defenders lacked the numbers to be able to defend the whole city, the government forces also did not have the strength both to hold their gains in Kramatorsk and also move against Sloviansk.

The 95th Airmobile Brigade

The emergence of the 95th Separate Airmobile Bde reflects the challenges Ukraine had building a new military after independence. Moscow withdrew a disproportionate share of the more elite Red Army units on the dissolution of the USSR, and although ethnic Ukrainians had been heavily represented in the paratroopers, there were limited structures in Ukraine – and even fewer resources to keep them manned and equipped. The brigade was originally established in 1993 as the 95th Training Centre for Junior Airmobile Troops Specialists in Zhytomyr, then being reorganized as the 95th Separate Airmobile Bde in 1996. Although a step forward in terms of operational capacity, this also represented part of the shrinkage taking place in the military, as the centre's five line battalions became just three. Subordinated to the 8th Army Corps, there was a real concern that it would simply become a glorified light infantry brigade, until the decision was made in 2012 to establish the Highly Mobile Landing Forces (VDV) as a separate arm of service, reflecting in part an awareness of the parlous state of the rest of the military. As one former paratrooper reminisced, 'more than anything, this was about saving us from drowning in the same swamp as the army', not least as it meant it was manned exclusively by volunteers. The 98th became part of the VDV, organized as three airmobile battalions, a howitzer artillery division and a tank company with T-80BVs. In 2015, it became the 95th Separate Abn Assault Bde.

Government soldiers in a BMP-2 IFV with pintle-mounted 9P135M anti-tank (AT) missile launcher hold a position on Kramatorsk's military airbase in April 2014. (Photo by Pierre Crom/Getty Images)

In what seems to have been a counter-productive waver, the next day, the government forces in Kramatorsk withdrew to the confines of the airport, and the main focus returned to Sloviansk. The militants were hard pressed, but were able to limit further government advances and down another Mi-24 with heavy machine gun fire. However, it was clear that they needed more supplies of ammunition and, ideally, manpower. On 12 May, when Strelkov was officially appointed DNR defence minister, he appealed to Moscow to 'take measures adequate to the situation to protect the population of the DNR, including the possibility of introducing a contingent of peacekeeping forces from the eastern border'. However, despite earlier claims (since debunked) from Ukrainian First Deputy Prime Minister Vitaly Yarema that elements of Russia's '45th Airborne Div' – presumably the 45th Guards Spetsnaz Rgt – had been deployed to Sloviansk, there was no suggestion from the Kremlin that it would be coming to join the conflict directly. The rebels were able to launch some local ambushes and attacks, including the successful interception of an ammunition convoy which saw seven paratroopers from the 95th Bde killed and an APC and a GAZ-66 mounting an 82mm mortar destroyed. It was clear, though, that the government forces were preparing for a new offensive.

On 18 May, supported by artillery and a pair of Su-25 attack aircraft, they launched a renewed assault along the Sloviansk–Kramatorsk axis. In tough fighting, the government forces, led by six BTR-70 APCs, were able to break into Kramatorsk and take the north-west of the city, before being blocked at a bridge over the Kazeny Torets River, as they came under sustained fire from rebels sheltering in the nearby Energomashspetsstal steel plant. Despite brief, and often disregarded, ceasefires, essentially this set the pattern for the next month, with the government forces launching small-scale attacks, which kept the rebels under pressure but were unable to make any substantive breakthrough into either city.

Nonetheless, the government forces were able to muster more troops and volunteers, especially from Right Sector, while the rebels, seeing the prospects of either a military victory or Russian assistance dwindle, began to experience greater problems maintaining

Rebel fighters stand guard outside the main administrative building in Sloviansk, on 16 April 2014. Behind them are the BMD-2 IFVs and 2S9 Nona gun-mortar of the 25th Airmobile Bde that either they had captured or which had been brought over by defecting government troops. (Photo by Olya Engalycheva/Anadolu Agency/Getty Images)

their already shaky discipline. Strelkov revived a decree of Stalin's on martial law, introduced in the midst of the Axis invasion in 1941, and three-man military tribunals to enforce it. On this basis, two rebel fighters – a company commander and a platoon sergeant – were executed for looting, as well as one resident of Sloviansk, while a fourth man, reportedly a Right Sector activist, was also sentenced to death for killing a rebel fighter. The militants' morale was briefly raised on 29 May, when they shot down an Mi-8 helicopter that was carrying National Guard Maj. Gen. Serhii Kulchitsky and six special police, but even Strelkov seems to have had some appreciation of the difficulty of his position, especially as the pro-government forces began to be able to make more use of their airpower. Despite an An-30 surveillance aircraft being shot down on 6 June, the Ukrainian air force was increasingly in evidence, and, on 14 June, what are believed to have been two Su-27 Flankers from the 39th Tactical Aviation Bde struck rebel positions in Kramatorsk with FAB-250 'iron bombs', killing or wounding dozens.

Ukraine's fleet of Su-27s, like this Su-27UB from the 831st Tactical Aviation Brigade based at Myrhorod Air Base, were able only to play a limited role in the campaign because of Russia's AA cover for the rebels. (Alan Wilson, CC BY-SA 2.0 https://creativecommons.org/licenses/by-sa/2.0, via Wikimedia Commons)

Under escalating pressure, on 5 July, the rebels withdrew from Sloviansk to Kramatorsk, and the same day Strelkov led a combined force from Kramatorsk south to Donetsk. According to him, 80–90 per cent of the rebel forces managed to extract themselves from Sloviansk. Kyiv later claimed it had let them withdraw because it thought the rebels may have been using civilians as human shields, although nationalists would later challenge this and accuse the government commanders of simply being too slow to act. Either way, though, this was a victory for Kyiv, even if both cities were left seriously damaged (almost half the local population had fled, either deeper into DNR-held territory, or west and north into loyalist regions).

THE RUSSIAN SPRING

However, even as government forces struggled to retake the city, Strelkov's seizure of Sloviansk had in many ways already proved a turning point in the so-called 'Russian Spring', a spate of other local risings and clashes across southern and eastern Ukraine, which local authorities – sometimes essentially in paralysis, sometimes sympathetic to the anti-Maidan forces – often struggled to contain. There was no central coordination, and the motives of protesters ranged from outright secessionism to, more often, a reaction to what they saw as hostility from the rest of the country. The new government in Kyiv was unsure how to respond and largely incapable of projecting power into the Donbas: in effect, between defections in the officer corps, fears about the reliability of units and years of neglect under Yanukovych, as of March, out of the notional 136,000 personnel in its Ground Forces, it could muster only perhaps 6,000 combat-ready troops (and they also had to guard Ukraine's borders and the Perekop Isthmus connecting the mainland with Russian-occupied Crimea). In the vacuum emerged a mix of local self-defence forces and out-and-out nationalist militias, every bit as mixed and

The Misanthropic Division

This paramilitary, neo-Nazi movement emerged in the early days of the Revolution of Dignity and soon spread its operations to Kharkiv and Odesa. As the Donbas conflict developed, it cohered into a series of smaller military units, together accounting for some 400 fighters, drawn both from Ukrainians and volunteers from Europe. It never really managed to establish a clear structure, though, and in practice remained within the orbit of first Right Sector and then Azov, not least because, as one former member admitted, it was 'more interested in fighting than organizing'. Its motto, *Töten für Wotan* (Killing for Odin), speaks to its Germanic and neo-Pagan identity.

out of control as on the rebel side. As extremists on both sides clashed, their respective supporters became radicalized.

Back in January, for example, the port city of Odesa had witnessed violence between supporters of the Maidan, who marched on the regional government buildings, and a combined force of those still backing the Yanukovych regime and local police. Tensions remained high, and extremists on both sides came to Odesa, including Russians associated with the neo-fascist Odesskaya Druzhina movement, and Ukrainian nationalists from Right Sector and the Misanthropic Division.

On 2 May, a rally in support of the new government was attacked by anti-Maidan activists, who asserted that they wanted not independence from Ukraine but greater autonomy, and an exchange of stones, petrol bombs and then gunfire ensued, with deaths on both sides. The anti-government elements had established a protest camp at Kulykove Polye square near the main railway station, and Ukrainian nationalists then attacked that. This drove some of the anti-government activists to take shelter in the nearby Trade Union House. When an attempt was made to storm it, the building caught fire as both sides traded petrol bombs. Forty-two people died in the blaze, with some alleging that the emergency services – which took 40 minutes to arrive, even though a fire station was 5 minutes away – were deliberately delayed. Ill feeling would persist between both camps, but the events of 2 May not only led to the imposition of martial law there but also shocked the anti-Maidan community, and Odesa would gradually be brought back into Kyiv's control.

Likewise, in Kharkiv, a statue of Bolshevik leader Lenin (whom, ironically enough, Putin blames for Ukraine's existence, as he transferred territories regarded as Russian under the old tsarist state to the new Ukrainian Soviet Socialist Republic) became a lightning rod for pro- and anti-Maidan protests in February. On 1 March, anti-Maidan activists stormed the Regional State Administration building, but the local government remained loyal to Kyiv. Escalating violence culminated on 14 March when Right Sector activists and members of Andriy Biletsky's Black Corps, in many ways a precursor to Azov, attacked an anti-Maidan rally, which led to gunfire and the use of

Police belatedly stand guard over the burnt-out Trade Union House in Odesa, where 40 anti-Maidan militants died. (Photo by ANATOLII STEPANOV/AFP via Getty Images)

A standoff between locals and government troops in Mariupol in May 2014. (Graham Phillips, CC BY 3.0 https://creativecommons.org/licenses/by/3.0, via Wikimedia Commons)

firebombs. Although several Right Sector fighters were arrested, the mood in the city crystallized against the anti-Maidan forces. Talk of a 'people's referendum' on the creation of a Kharkiv People's Republic went nowhere, and Mayor Hennady Hernes and the heads of the local security agencies (as well as wealthy local businessmen who were willing to bankroll their own gangs of street toughs) were united in their repudiation of any rebellion.

Like Kharkiv, the port city of Mariupol had been a stronghold of Yanukovych's Party of Regions and from February witnessed protests both in support of and in opposition to the Revolution of Dignity. Although local politician Dmitry Kuzmenko was hailed as the 'people's mayor' by protesters opposed to the new government, again the balance of power tilted against them. Kuzmenko was arrested. On 13 April, around a thousand protesters were able to seize the city administration building, which they then barricaded, but a subsequent attempt to occupy an Interior Troops base was repelled with gunfire. The insurgents appeared to be trying to capture weapons, but with the arrival of Omega Group commandos their attempts were foiled. Meanwhile, loyalist volunteer forces such as the Mariupol People's Militia began to emerge in response.

On 3 May, these tensions escalated into armed violence, largely between militias. By this stage, especially thanks to extensive funding from billionaire oligarch Ihor Kolomoisky – who was supporting a range of these volunteer battalions – Biletsky had spun up a new unit, which was formally called the Azov Special Tasks Patrol Police Bn. Given the desperate state of the ZSU, in April, Interior Minister Arsen Avakov had issued a decree regularizing volunteer battalions of up to 12,000 personnel within the Special Tasks Patrol Police. They still largely handled their own recruitment, training and fundraising, but this was a first step in Kyiv's attempts to take control of

Dnipro-1

Another of the Special Tasks Patrol Police battalions, Dnipro-1 was very much one of Ihor Kolomoisky's projects, and he spent a reported $10 million to raise and equip it, in April 2014, after Kyiv had appointed him governor of Dnipropetrovsk region. It initially gathered some 400 men in the city of Dnipro (formerly known as Dnipropetrovsk) who received just a week's basic training before deployment. Their first serious engagement was in Mariupol, and they would later take serious losses in Ilovaisk, but, by the end of 2014, they had been expanded to a strength of 600, in five companies, four of which were essentially motorized infantry, and the 1st Armoured Company (Coy), which fielded BTR APCs.

the militias, without strangling them. The Azov Bn was originally based at Berdyansk, 75km along the coast to the west, but as volunteers from the DNR and LNR arrived in Mariupol, Azov also joined the fray. For over a month, pro- and anti-government forces clashed sporadically, occasionally lethally. The police headquarters was burnt down when government forces tried to retake it from a mix of rebellious police and their allies. The DNR authorities appointed one Andrei Borisov (known as Chechen) as 'city commander' but he was later chased out by Azov fighters. By mid-June, the anti-government forces had largely been controlled or expelled from the city, with Azov and another volunteer battalion, Dnipro-1 at the fore.

KYIV STRIKES BACK

By May–June, then, the rough outlines of the conflict had emerged. Although the 'front lines' were hazy and mutable, insurgents had taken Donetsk and Luhansk, and from them established their self-proclaimed 'people's republics' in the central Donbas. Attempts to raise rebellion along the coast between Mariupol and Odesa had failed, as had efforts farther west, in Kharkiv, Dnipro and Zaporizhia. Even so, this was still a confused situation. Donetsk Airport, for example, was still in government hands, even though the city was the heart of the rebel DNR. Furthermore, despite the rebels' efforts to portray their insurgencies as a response to a Ukrainian-speaking majority trying to persecute a Russian-speaking minority, the militias that had emerged on both sides were, at this time, equally drawn from the Russian-speakers of eastern Ukraine.

In May, the leaders of the self-proclaimed republics announced that they were forming a confederation known as Novorossiya (New Russia) with Strelkov as their defence minister. They seemed to have assumed that Moscow would defend, underwrite and bankroll a new nation. Despite a certain amount of support from some quarters within the Russian elite, this was absolutely not on the cards. However, Putin did accede to the covert provision of limited supplies of heavy weapons to bolster the rebels' arsenals, and also a small-scale introduction of intelligence officers, trainers and

Until Moscow was willing to provide substantial amounts of aid, the rebels were often forced to scavenge and improvise, such as with this crudely armoured gun-truck mounting a ZSU-23-2 AA gun, seen in DNR service. (Photo by Pierre Crom/Getty Images)

specialists, again on an undercover basis. Soldiers who wanted to volunteer to fight alongside the rebels were allowed to 'go on holiday', usually with their personal weapons.

This would all prove increasingly necessary, because on 1 May, Kyiv reintroduced conscription (which Yanukovych had ended the year before), as it finally began mustering its forces for a concerted campaign in the Donbas. The election of Petro Poroshenko as president on 25 May helped resolve the uncertainty within the government and opened the way for a more active approach to the war. The ATO command became an increasingly authoritative structure (even if there would be considerable criticism directed at its strategy, especially by volunteer battalions who felt it was too hidebound). The area of operations was divided into four sectors: A, B, S and D. Sectors A, D and B ran north to south along the Russian border, from above Luhansk down to Mariupol on the Azov Sea coast. Sector S spread across a wide area to the rear of the others, including Sloviansk and Kramatorsk. Sector commanders were given greater freedom of operation – even though overall this was still envisaged as quite a hierarchical structure – and more men and materiel began flowing into the Donbas.

Moscow had already demonstrated that it was beginning to be concerned that its local allies and would-be proxies were both out of control and not up to the job. In May, a new player had arrived in Donetsk: the Vostok (East) Bn. This was originally raised largely by the GU from fighters from the North Caucasus, although once deployed it was quickly 'Ukrainianized' and put under Alexander Khodakovsky's control. Its first act, as a demonstrative reminder that the locals needed to remember that Moscow was their patron and ultimate master, was the seizure of the local administration building, which the DNR's leaders had been using as their HQ. The replacement of fighters from the Russian Federation with Ukrainian recruits before it was deployed against pro-government forces, though, was a sign that the Kremlin was still eager to try and minimize its role in the conflict.

It would not long be able to maintain this distance, as the war turned against the rebels. That Donetsk International Airport, just 10km north-west of the city, remained in government hands had been an embarrassment for the DNR leadership and also a potential vulnerability. So long as the rebels had enough AA assets that landing forces there would be extremely risky, the thought that Kyiv might find a way of using it to launch an attack remained a concern. On 26 May, a 200-strong DNR force including the Vostok Bn, Russian Orthodox Army and Iskra (Spark), a platoon-sized unit of Russian volunteers, managed to take the terminal buildings, but Ukrainian paratroopers and National Guard soon launched a fierce counter-attack, supported from the air by Mi-24 gunships and Su-25 attack aircraft. The helicopters suppressed DNR AA assets with rockets and

Soldiers from the 'new model' Vostok Bn after it had been remanned with the pick of local recruits, standing guard in Donetsk, with their BTR-60PB APC in the background. (Photo by Brendan Hoffman/ Getty Images)

Government soldiers with an SPG-9 73mm recoilless rifle near Donetsk Airport. The SPG-9 was a dated weapon, even then, but still useful in the relative absence of more modern anti-armour weapons. (Photo by Viktor Koshkin/ Anadolu Agency/Getty Images)

missiles, allowing the Su-25s to target the rebels. Even a KS-19 100mm AA gun was pressed into service in a direct fire role, battering the terminal buildings while the rebels had only a single AGS-17 30mm automatic grenade launcher (AGL) as an inadequate counter. Some operators from Russia's 10th Spetsnaz Bde were reportedly rushed in to reinforce the defenders, a mark of how seriously the Russians saw the situation as they were largely trying to avoid being sucked into combat operations. Even so, by the next day, the DNR forces had been pushed back out of the airport, and the DNR military leadership humiliated. Indeed, when the Vostok contingent had tried to make its way back into Donetsk in two KamAZ trucks, it was fired upon with grenade launchers and machine guns by other rebels, who assumed it was Ukrainian National Guards launching an attack on the city: Khodakovsky and Borodai would subsequently trade bitter accusations of blame that led to a split that was never properly healed.

The bad news for the rebels accumulated. The same weekend that Sloviansk and Kramatorsk fell, so too did Druzhkivka, Kostiantynivka and Artemivsk (from 2016 known as Bakhmut, the site of one of the bloodiest battles of the later full-scale Russian invasion), pushing the front line perilously close to Horlivka, which straddled the strategic E50/M04 highway link between Donetsk and Luhansk. Rebel unity and morale was looking fragile, with recriminations emerging as to who was to blame for the spate of defeats in early July.

Artemivsk and the battle for arsenals

The seizure of much of Artemivsk in April by forces under Igor Bezler had been especially significant because it was the site of the 1282nd Centre for Armoured Weapon Provision, with stocks of decommissioned but still usable armoured vehicles: some 260 T-64, T-72 and T-80 tanks and a larger number of APCs and IFVs. In addition, the nearby village of Paraskoviivka housed a small arms arsenal. As a result, the skirmishes in and around Artemivsk were unusual in the use of tanks on both sides. The loyalists were able to deploy a T-64 and a BMP-2 IFV from the 1282nd's stocks, while the rebels had at least one T-64BV. Although the claim was made that this had been provided by Russia, the rebels asserted that it had come from loyalist stocks. Thanks especially to the efforts of the army's 3rd Special Forces Rgt under Col. Olexander Trepak, neither the 1282nd Centre nor the Paraskoviivka armoury fell into rebel hands.

Moscow had expected more of the people of the Donbas to support the anti-government movements, stirred up by a propaganda campaign that portrayed the new leadership in Kyiv as at best hostile to Russian-speakers, at worst neo-Nazi. It had looked at the demoralized and badly equipped military (and the way so many units in Crimea had switched sides or simply retreated) and assumed they would not be willing or able to fight. It had encouraged militias to emerge on the rebel side, not imagining that a combination of genuine patriotism and oligarch money would help pro-Kyiv militias emerge, too. In other words, and not for the first time, Putin had seriously underestimated the Ukrainians.

Nonetheless, Moscow continued to try and limit its involvement, even while supporting the rebels. It was still not willing to deploy its own forces openly, but already by the end of June had begun trickling in heavier weapons such as self-propelled guns and AA missiles to counter the government's advantage in artillery and airpower. It also moved to try and assert greater control over the fractious rebels, with more of the 'volunteers' from Russia taking up command positions being regular army and GU officers under a veil of deniability.

THE SHOOTING DOWN OF MH17

This would lead to a tragedy that in many ways came to define the conflict and ultimately force Moscow to intervene directly. Russia had been providing a degree of AA cover to the rebels from systems located on its own territory, as well as a supply of MANPADS. One of these appears to have been used to down an Il-76 military transport carrying 40 paratroopers, on approach to Luhansk Airport on 14 June, although a Buk M1 (SA-11) surface-to-air missile system was likely used from over the border to shoot down an An-26 transport, also over Luhansk, a month later. The rebels had claimed that they had captured a Buk from government forces and used that, but this is disputed.

The indictment of Nazarov

When the Il-76 transport from the 25th Transport Aviation Bde was shot down over Luhansk on 14 June 2014, this became something of a political scandal. It had been part of a three-aircraft wing ferrying reinforcements to government-held Luhansk Airport, carrying 40 paratroopers from the 25th Abn Bde, but despite the use of flares fired to blind and decoy the seeker warhead, it was hit and shot down by a 9K38 Igla shoulder-fired missile, killing all on board. This was the largest single loss of lives since the start of the conflict – and the largest for the ZSU since independence. An outraged Ukrainian public wanted some satisfaction, and unable to visit this on the rebels, instead turned on their own. In November, it emerged that the SBU was investigating ATO commander Maj. Gen. Nazarov on charges of gross negligence. He was formally arrested on 25 November, although bailed out two days later. The SBU's claim was that they had warned him of the risk of a 'terrorist attack' – Nazarov's defenders responded that the SBU was constantly passing on numerous and vague warnings, and that this flight had been both operationally necessary and a reasonable risk. A first hearing was held on 7 December and even broadcast live on the internet. On 27 March 2017, Nazarov was found guilty and sentenced to seven years in prison, although a stay was granted for him to appeal. In 2020, the Dnipro Court of Appeal rejected this and upheld the original sentence, but this was overturned the next year by the Supreme Court. While in itself this case ended up going nowhere, the whole saga was symbolic of the often-tense relationship between the military and the SBU but also the degree to which Ukrainian public opinion was still unable to understand how war had come to the Donbas – or been allowed to – and this confusion sometimes led to a search for scapegoats.

SHOOTING DOWN MH17, 17 JULY 2014 (PP.54–55)

As rebel fighters from the Donetsk Republican Guard look on, distinguishable by their 'Novorossiya' sleeve patches **(1)**, one of the 9M317 surface-to-air missiles on a Buk M1-2 launcher **(2)** blasts into the sky. Instead of the Ukrainian government aircraft the rebels thought they had detected, its target was a civilian airliner, a Boeing 777-200ER flown by Malaysia Airlines, with 298 passengers and crew. Moscow had provided the rebels with the launch units, which have their own simpler radars, but not the battery command and target acquisition radar vehicles, whose greater sensor and computing capacity might have distinguished an airliner that was very slightly off its standard flight lane from a military transport. Homing in at Mach 3, the missile detonated on its final approach, riddling the civilian aircraft with shrapnel. It crashed nearby, killing everyone on board. When the rebels – and the Russians who had supplied these powerful AA systems – realized their mistake, a massive cover-up was launched. Nonetheless, it very quickly became clear that this tragedy had been perpetrated by the rebels, armed by Moscow.

Regardless, on 17 July, the Russians did covertly transfer three Buk launch systems to the rebels, each with a full complement of four missiles, in an operation overseen by Col. Gen. 'Delfin' Tkachyov. These were passed on to DNR intelligence officer Leonid 'Krot' Kharchenko, albeit probably with 'volunteer' crews from the Russian 53rd AA Missile Bde. Later that day, Malaysia Airlines Flight 17 (MH17) was on a scheduled run from Amsterdam to Kuala Lumpur. Although some airlines had rerouted any flights that crossed the Donbas, many – like Malaysia Airlines – had not, as there had been no threats to civilian air traffic. The Boeing 777-200ER was about 50km from the Russian–Ukrainian border when it suddenly disappeared from radar. It had been shot down, and all 298 passengers and crew were killed, the wreckage raining down near the village of Hrabove.

Although the Russian disinformation machine quickly cranked into high gear, churning out alternative explanations from the technically unfeasible (such as that it was shot down by a Ukrainian Su-25, which could not have flown high enough to manage this) to the surreal (that it was all a CIA plot, stuffed with corpses and deliberately crashed to discredit the rebels), the basic facts of the situation would soon become clear. According to Russian practice, Buks would be fielded in battalions comprising a command vehicle, a specialized radar vehicle, six transporter erector launcher and radar (TELAR) vehicles and three transporter erector launcher (TEL) vehicles. The Russians had provided the rebels with just three TELARs and crews, and while these mounted their own fire control radars, they lacked the more advanced capabilities the specialist systems offered. Command over the launchers had been handed to the rebels, and when the Buks' radars picked up a large target flying eastwards, they clearly leapt to the conclusion that it was another Ukrainian An-26 transport or reconnaissance aircraft. It is unclear whether Strelkov or Sergei 'Khmury' Dubinsky, the head of DNR military intelligence, gave orders for the target to be engaged – the only evidence yet uncovered has been an excited message from Kharchenko to Dubinsky, that they had already shot down one Ukrainian aircraft. Indeed, after the crash, Strelkov appears to have accepted this account, issuing

The still-burning wreckage of MH17 in a field outside Hrabove, eastern Donbas. (Photo by Pierre Crom/ Getty Images)

a later-deleted social media post crowing that 'in the region of Torez, an An-26 plane has been shot down, somewhere near the "Progress" mine. We warned them not to fly "in our sky". Here is video evidence of yet another "bird fall".' This was picked up by the Russian news outlet *LifeNews* that reported that the shooting down of a 'Ukrainian Air Force An-26 transport plane' was 'a new victory for the Donetsk militia'. This, too, was later scrubbed from the site.

Immediately after the shooting down of MH17, at least two of the Buks – one of which was seen to be missing one of its 9M317 missiles – were hurriedly withdrawn back to Russia, although not without being seen and captured on camera. Nonetheless, this was not just a blunder and tragedy, it was also a lesson for Moscow. Simply handing increasingly powerful weapons to rebels who often lacked the technical expertise and impulse control to use them wisely, weapons which, when misused could all too easily be tracked back to Russia, was neither enough to turn the tide of war nor did it grant the kind of plausible deniability the Kremlin had been seeking. A Western military attaché based in Moscow at the time noted that 'although no one wanted to admit it publicly, it was getting closer to put up or shut up time'.

STRANGLING THE REBELLIONS

The Kremlin was sliding into ever more obvious support of the rebels. On 27 July, the US government released satellite photographs demonstrating that long-range BM-27 Uragan 220mm MLRSs were being used from Russian territory to attack Ukrainian government targets. Meanwhile, 'Orion' – Lt. Gen. Ivannikov – was negotiating the provision of a 2S19 152mm Msta-S SPG and a number of MT-LB gun tractors with 2S12 120mm mortars.

This was not enough, though, as the government forces were proving more confident, coherent and aggressive by the day. One of the most striking operations in this phase of the war was the raid carried out by the 95th

A Ukrainian soldier manning a turret-mounted DShK heavy machine gun. (Photo by Viktor Koshkin/Anadolu Agency/Getty Images)

Ukrainian paratroopers atop their 2S9 Nona 120mm self-propelled gun-mortar, while refugees board a train to take them westwards, out of the combat zone. (Photo by Olga Engalycheva/Anadolu Agency/Getty Images)

Airmobile Bde between 19 July and 10 August. The aim was to try and soften up the rebel rear for future efforts to cut off the DNR and LNR from Russia and more immediately to relieve elements of the 24th and 72nd Mech and 79th Air Assault Bdes, whose lines of potential retreat had been cut off by rebel forces. Under 95th Bde commander (and future ATO commander) Col. Mykhailo Zabrodsky, a 500-strong task force was established at Kramatorsk at the end of June, which also included contingents from the 30th and 51st Mech and 25th Abn Bdes. On 19 July, they moved east to rebel-held Lysychansk, where they took a commanding height over the town in a pincer movement that allowed them to secure a nearby oil refinery and then strike at militants in the town itself. The task force was meant to keep moving, so while the Donbas Bn took over the job of clearing the remaining militants in Lysychansk, it headed south-west to Artemivsk, then south-east to Krasny Luch via Debaltseve. From there, they skirted Luhansk, sweeping away rebel checkpoints and causing panic among the LNR leadership, before returning to Kramatorsk. This was a raid in force, a 470km sweep that succeeded in disrupting and demoralizing the rebels and opening a route for some 3,000 Ukrainian soldiers and militiamen to escape encirclement. As such, it was a powerful fillip for Ukrainian morale and also a mark of the growing confidence of the government forces.

More to the point, Kyiv was now able to plan operations intended to separate Donetsk and Luhansk physically from each other, and from the border with Russia, across which flowed increasingly vital supplies of men and materiel. By the beginning of August, the rebel-held portions of Donetsk and Luhansk regions had been reduced to some 40 per cent of the total, and Kyiv's forces were more able to interdict movements within, as well as between, the DNR and LNR. The decision was made to strike first at Ilovaisk and then Debaltseve, respectively, between Donetsk and the Russian border and between Donetsk and Luhansk, as targets for new offensives, with which to cut a corridor across the rebel territory. This would also have the virtue of moving the front line farther from the border and easing the pressure on the ATO's Sector D. Despite efforts to widen the 'airgap' between the rebels and

In this often small-scale conflict, checkpoints like this one at Perevalsk, guarded by LNR Cossacks, would often assume outsized importance for their role blocking supply lines and symbolically asserting control to areas which were not otherwise really controlled by the forces in question. (Photo by Brendan Hoffman/ Getty Images)

the Russians, especially the narrow stretches between the Ukrainian villages of Saurinka and Dmytrivka to the south of the sector, and Vosnesenivka and Izvaryne to the north, it was still all but impossible to secure this territory because the Russians were able to bombard government forces and jam their communications from their side of the frontier.

Lt. Gen. Petro Lytvyn, the commander of Sector D, had a mix of forces at his disposal, including two battalions of the 30th Mech Bde, one battalion each from the 51st Mech Bde and 25th and 95th Airmobile Bdes, as well as a volunteer unit from western Ukraine, the 5th 'Prykarpattya' TDB. However, although the goal was to take rebel settlements one by one, first encircling them from all sides, and then launching an assault at an opportune moment, to secure a base for the next extension and thus extend the secure zone, the progress made in practice was often temporary. On 27 July, for example, the 5th Bn, supported by National Guard volunteers, advanced into Shakhtarsk, deeper into DNR territory, and established a slightly shaky control over the town. However, within a couple of days, bolstered by reinforcements from nearby Snizhne, the rebels had retaken the town, or at least its now-deserted remnants, with the government troops forced to retreat under heavy mortar fire. This was despite the rare use of three OTR-21 Tochka tactical ballistic missiles against DNR concentrations near Snizhne.

On 3 August, Kyiv announced that its troops had finally severed the last connections between the DNR and LNR, and although this proved premature, it did highlight a serious concern for Moscow. If government forces could close the border, then they could throttle off the supply of fighters, weapons and ammunition. This would force Moscow's hand: while it could still bombard the government forces from across the border, this would not be enough to save the rebels. Unsurprisingly, already there were hints that some of the militant leaders were seeking either to flee to Russia or make their own deals with Kyiv. Moscow's choice was thus to escalate or withdraw. It chose to escalate, abandoning any hope that deniable proxies with minimal assistance could hold their own against an increasingly confident alliance of government troops and militias. The Kremlin may not have started this rebellion, but having decided to try and co-opt it, it was not willing to let it be defeated.

THE ILOVAISK CAULDRON

In early August, government forces under Lt. Gen. Ruslan Khomchak, commander of Sector B, were closing on Ilovaisk, a strategic road and railway junction, which had been in rebel hands since April. His army was a mix of regular and volunteer battalions, and would suffer from challenges coordinating often disparate units. Nonetheless, Khomchak was confident, as his intelligence section reassured him that there were no more than 80 lightly armed militiamen left in the city. Initially, he tasked the 40th 'Kryvbas' TDB with investing the city. However, this was a volunteer unit, fresh from training, and while it was formally part of the ZSU, it was severely lacking in both experienced soldiers and heavier weapons. Its commander, Col. Motriya, was also unconvinced that the city was so poorly defended. First he and his intelligence officer appealed to Khomchak to think again, and then when he refused to change his orders, flatly refused.

This was just as well for the 40th Bn, as the defenders actually amounted to several hundred fighters from the Oplot and Sparta Bns, including a few T-64 tanks and at least one S-60 57mm AA gun, which, while a dated design, could still be deadly when used in a direct fire role, and a 2S1 Gvozdika 122mm SPG. Even more dangerous in an urban setting were the four AGS-17 automatic grenade launchers that the Oplot fighters had brought with them.

In any case, an infuriated Khomchak had to pause and bring up further forces. By 9 August, he had assembled some 400 men from the Donbas, Dnipro-1, Shakhtarsk and Azov Bns, who launched a first assault on Ilovaisk the next day. They were also supported by three artillery pieces and three T-64 tanks from the army's 51st 'Volyn' Separate Mech Bde. This proved of little real value, though: one tank broke down, one never deployed, and

Until the advent of Russian forces, one area where the government forces did have the advantage was in armour, but too often these forces would be dispersed or found themselves in the adverse environment of street fighting. (Ministry of Defence of Ukraine, CC BY-SA 2.0 https://creativecommons.org/licenses/by-sa/2.0, via Wikimedia Commons)

A Russian paratrooper; note the additional sight added to his AKM-74 rifle. (Ilya Varlamov, CC BY-SA 4.0 https://creativecommons.org/licenses/by-sa/4.0, via Wikimedia Commons)

one was quickly knocked out by the rebel 2S1. Nonetheless, the government forces were able to break through the city's outer defences, but then they found themselves in a messy urban fight, facing harassing sniper and RPG fire from higher floors and having trouble coordinating their operations. Indeed, reportedly a Russian Spetsnaz team was present and managed to infiltrate between the Donbas and Azov elements, almost managing to provoke them into exchanging friendly fire. The attack petered out, and the government forces, shaken and lacking the strength either to take the centre of the city or hold the territory they had taken, withdrew.

Now rather more chastened, Khomchak realized he was going to need more men and more firepower. He brought in a company from the Myrotvorets Bn, and a platoon each from 21st Kherson TDB and the Svityaz and Ivano-Frankivsk Coys of the Liut Bde. While a company from the 51st Bde and two platoons from the 17th 'Kryvyi Rih' Tank Bde secured the city limits to prevent the arrival of reinforcements, and 2S1s from the 51st Bde provided fire support, the volunteers would storm the city. Meanwhile, elements of the 93rd 'Dnipropetrovsk' Mech Bde were nearing the city, in case further assistance was required.

It was. The volunteers, eventually supplemented by at least a company from the 93rd Bde, were able to take the neighbourhoods west of the railway line that cut the city north to south by 18 August and it now seemed just a matter of mopping up, even though some reinforcements from Donetsk, drawn from the Vostok and Oplot Bns, were able to make their way to join the defenders. The news that, farther from the city, the militants had been able to seize Savur-Mohyla, a strategic hill to the east, seemed of little relevance. Neither Khomchak nor Lytvyn seemed to give it much notice. However, not only was this useful high ground for emplacing and spotting for artillery, its capture opened a breach in the Ukrainians' defensive perimeter: the road from Russia was again open. This mattered because the Kremlin had made a momentous decision: Ilovaisk could not be allowed to fall.

Elements of the 6th Tank Bde, the 8th Guards and 18th MR Bdes and paratroopers from the 31st Guards Air Assault Bde had been brought to full combat status. Each brigade generated a battalion tactical group (BTG), a support-heavy manoeuvre unit drawn only from professionals (not least as Russian law bans the deployment of conscripts abroad without a formal declaration of war), while dedicated intervention units including the 137th Abn, 247th Air Assault and 331st Abn Rgts, which had been on stand-by since at least July, were also ready for deployment.

On 23 August, up to 100 Russian AFVs, led by the T-72BA tanks of the 6th Tank Bde, crossed the border. The DPSU in Kyiv and Sector D's command staff both alerted the ATO HQ, but the overall commander, Maj. Gen. Viktor Nazarov, dismissed the reports out of hand. Reports reached Khomchak the next day, but it is unclear whether he believed them. Either way, with Nazarov unconcerned, he continued to focus on pushing forward in Ilovaisk. Meanwhile, the evidence was mounting. Two officers from the 93rd Bde, hearing rumours, changed into civilian clothes and drove past the column, being greeted cheerily by Russian soldiers who assumed they were pro-rebel. When they reported this to the ATO command, they were told this must actually have been a government convoy. Sector D Chief of Staff Col. Petro Romihaylo went and observed the Russian advance himself, but when he passed on his report to Chief of the General Staff Lt. Gen. Viktor Muzhenko, he was airily assured that these were 'just demonstrative actions'. Although on 6 August, the National Security and Defence Council had announced that there was a possibility of a Russian military invasion and that the Ukrainian army was ready for it, when it actually happened, no one in the ATO and ZSU command structures was willing to believe it.

No one on the ground was as sanguine. The first unit in the Russians' path, Lytvyn's 5th 'Prykarpattya' TDB, simply broke as they approached on the 23rd, leaving a 40km hole in the Ukrainians' defensive line. This, in turn, left the flank of a company of the 28th Mech Bde exposed, made up of recently mobilized reservists who themselves largely opted to abandon their positions. By that night, the Russians were in a position to engage the Ukrainians mired in Ilovaisk from the south, and by the next were beginning to use their superior strength and firepower to inch around them, risking a full encirclement. Elements of the 'Kryvbas' TDB were forced to withdraw from positions outside the city, opening the way to envelopment, while another volunteer unit, the 2nd Horyn TDB, pre-emptively withdrew before the Russian advance, opening the road also for reinforcements for Ilovaisk from Donetsk, although a first attempt to use this to send forces to flank the besiegers was countered by a battalion from the 51st Mech Bde, near the village of Styla to the south of Donetsk.

However, the entire tactical situation had changed. Taking Ilovaisk now looked near-enough impossible and, more to the point, irrelevant. Khomchak neither had nor was willing to claim the authority to order a withdrawal, and while he feverishly petitioned the ATO command for permission to extricate his forces, for days he was told to hold fast and await reinforcements. The flipside of the Ukrainians' fierce desire to defend their territory was, as during the later full-scale war from 2022, sometimes a refusal to withdraw from untenable positions quickly enough. By 27 August, Ilovaisk was surrounded by the Russians, supplies and ammunition were running low and no reinforcements were forthcoming. Many Ukrainians fought hard and well, but they were simply outmatched. That day, a reinforced company from the 92nd Mech Bde was sent to try and force a breach in the Russian

A rebel fighter in front of an armoured vehicle taken from government forces during the battle of Ilovaisk. (Photo by MENAHEM KAHANA/AFP via Getty Images)

line, supported by volunteers from the 42nd Rukh Oporu TDB. Even before the two units had managed to connect, though, they were each engaged, first by accurate mortar and artillery fire and then by paratroopers from the 31st Air Assault Bde, and forced to withdraw having taken heavy casualties.

In what was an implicit acknowledgement of Russia's role, on 29 August, Putin himself announced that a 'humanitarian corridor' ought to be opened to allow the government forces to leave. DNR Prime Minister Zakharchenko hurriedly agreed. At this stage, Khomchak was in a bind. Kyiv was neither approving nor rejecting the deal, and he had 1,600 men trapped in a hostile city between the defenders and perhaps 4,000 relatively elite Russians. He did reject the initial demand that they lay down all their arms, but eventually agreed that they would abandon their armoured vehicles and heavy weapons. At 0600hrs on 29 August, the Ukrainian forces began withdrawing from Ilovaisk, heading south along the T0507 road to the outlying village of Mnohopillya. There, as agreed with the Russians, they divided into two columns, codenamed *Bulava* (Mace) and *Viter* (Wind).

What follows is still hotly debated. To the Ukrainians, it was a cynical and ruthless Russian ambush. The Russians, conversely, claim that the Ukrainians failed to observe the agreed routes and also broke the agreement by retaining their armoured vehicles. DNR Defence Minister Vladimir Kononov said: 'This morning, a number of armed units of the Ukrainian army began moving to break out of the encirclement. Some in armoured vehicles, some on foot… These actions have nothing to do with the humanitarian corridor.' It is generally recognized that the government forces were accompanied by armoured vehicles, including a captured Russian T-72BA, but the subsequent practices of the Russians in the Donbas make it hard not to suspect this was a trap rather than tragic miscommunication. In any case, after about an hour, *Bulava*, the column commanded by Khomchak himself, came under Russian fire, notably by a battery of D-30 howitzers of the 1065th Artillery Rgt. *Viter* made only a few kilometres southwards before being engaged at the village of Chervonosilske by the 6th Tank Bde and 31st Air Assault Bde. Despite hard fighting, they were able to hold the village until the next day, when Col. Yuri Lysenko, commander of the Dnipro-2 Bn and of the column as a whole, was able to negotiate their transfer to government-held territory under the auspices of the Red Cross.

By 1 September, Ilovaisk was back in rebel hands, more than 360 government troops and militia were dead, 429 wounded and more than 300 captured, and a new stage of the war had begun. Ukrainian Defence Minister Heletey declared that the country was fighting a 'full-scale Russian invasion'. The so-called 'Northern Wind' – direct intervention by Moscow – was blowing.

THE 'NORTHERN WIND'

There had already been small commitments of special forces, trainers and specialists, accompanying the so-called 'vacationers', the genuine volunteers who were allowed to go and serve in the Donbas – with kit and weapons – on the fiction that they were merely taking leave. Many of these 'vacationers' were simply rank-and-file fighters, but among them were special forces operators, from the 2nd and 10th Spetsnaz Bdes and the 45th Guards Abn Spetsnaz Rgt, who were there to provide close security for the more senior Russian advisers embedded within the LNR and DNR, but also a range of technical capabilities, from forward observers to sappers.

Only in December 2015 did Putin himself finally admit that there were Russian personnel in the Donbas (although, even then, he denied that they were there to fight, just, as he vaguely put it, 'resolving various issues'). Nonetheless, Moscow was clearly now willing to cast off its pretence of non-involvement and deploy full combat units. Even so, this was still seen simply as an occasional and situational response rather than a full-scale involvement. The Russians had deployed some 6,500 troops into Ukraine in August, and this would grow to a peak of some 10,000 by the end of the year, but often BTGs or artillery battalions and batteries would be deployed into the Donbas when needed to support an assault or, more often, shore up DNR and LNR defences against a government offensive, then be withdrawn back to Russia.

While the government forces had been able to win victories against the poorly disciplined and uncoordinated rebel militias, Kyiv had no illusions about its ability to resist Russian forces. Meanwhile, international concern

The more the Russians were involved, the more important it became for both sides to 'spin' the story to international audiences. Here, journalists interview soldiers from the loyalist Donbas Bn. (Лionкiнг, CC BY-SA 4.0 https://creativecommons.org/licenses/by-sa/4.0, via Wikimedia Commons)

THE BATTLE OF ILOVAISK, 7 AUGUST–2 SEPTEMBER 2014

The battle of Ilovaisk would prove a particular turning point, as it marked the first overt and substantive deployment of Russian regular forces into the Donbas, turning what had looked like a successful operation by government troops into a convincing defeat.

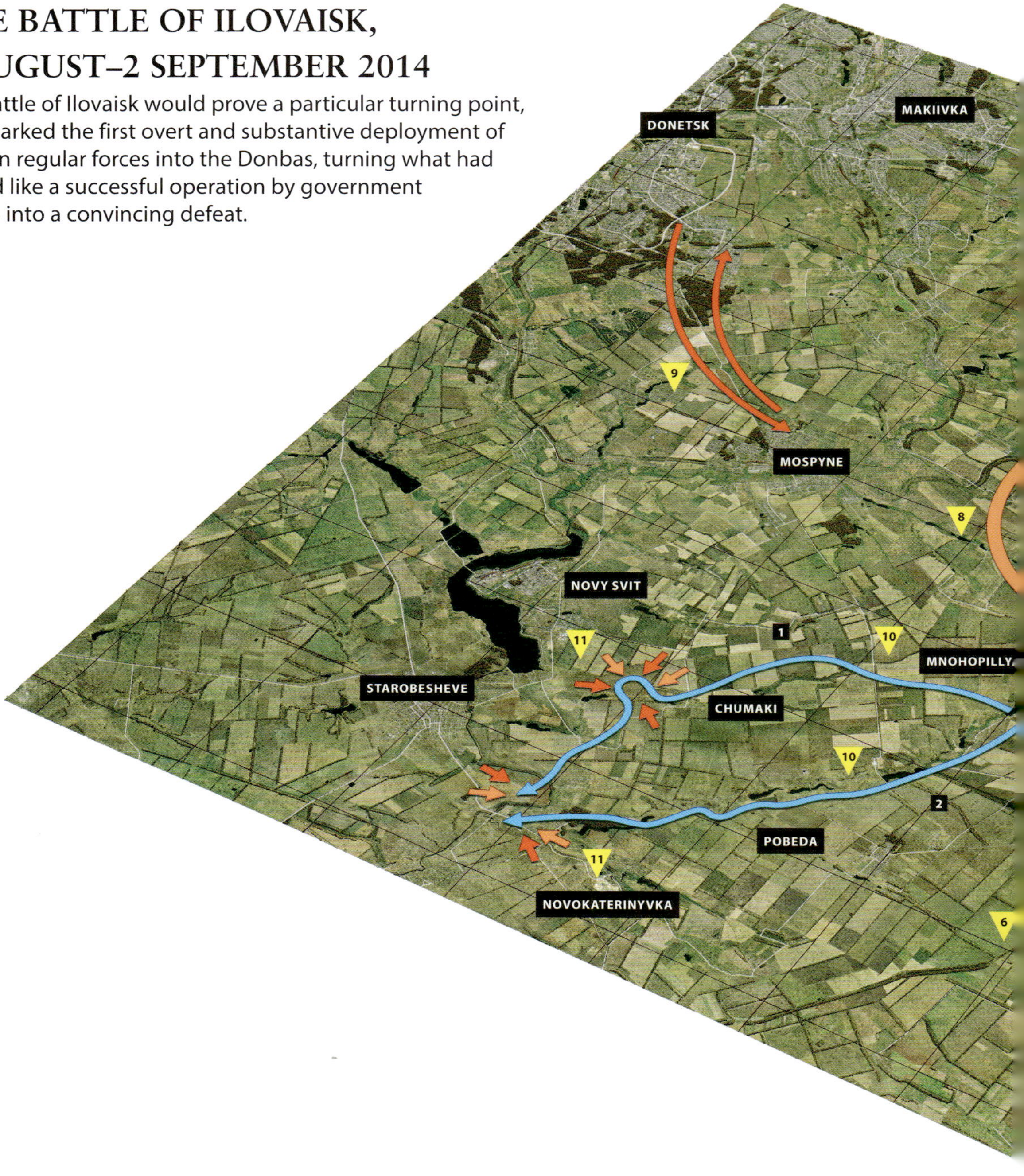

EVENTS

1. 27–29 July: Government forces from Sector D driven back from Shakhtarsk
2. 10 August: First government assault on Ilovaisk
3. 12–18 August: Second assault on Ilovaisk
4. 18 August: Rebels take Savur-Mohyla
5. 23 August: Vanguard of Russian forces (led by BTG of 6th Tank Bde) cross the border
6. 23 August: 5th TDB breaks
7. 24 August: Russians begin to encircle government troops engaged at Ilovaisk
8. 25–28 August: Russians, supported by rebels, close on government troops
9. 26 August: First rebel attempt to reinforce Ilovaisk blocked by 51st Mech Bde
10. 29 August: Withdrawal of government forces in columns *Bulava* **(1)** and *Viter* **(2)**
11. 29 August: Government forces engaged by rebels and Russians
12. 31 August–1 September: Ilovaisk fully reoccupied by rebels

Note: gridlines are shown at intervals of 5km (3.11 miles).

about the widening of the conflict was growing. At an informal meeting of heads of state at the commemoration of the 70th anniversary of the D-Day landings in Normandy on 6 June 2014, the decision had been made to establish a format to encourage dialogue between Kyiv and Moscow. The first meeting of this Trilateral Contact Group had taken place in Kyiv two days later, moderated by a representative of the Organization for Security and Co-operation in Europe (OSCE). They discussed a 15-point peace plan proposed by Poroshenko, but the Russians – sticking to their assertions of the time that they were not actual participants in this conflict – insisted the DNR and LNR also needed to be represented. The result was a series of meetings that, to be blunt, did little to advance any meaningful peace.

By the end of July, though, the pace had quickened a little, and meetings began to be held in the Belarusian capital, Minsk. French president François Hollande and German chancellor Angela Merkel were increasingly personally involved in trying to hammer out some kind of agreement, but for some time Kyiv was resistant to anything which might look like serious political concessions to the rebels. After Ilovaisk, though, Poroshenko realized that his options had suddenly become more limited – and both Hollande and Merkel, arguably more eager to see a deal which might forestall deeper Russian intervention than to safeguard Ukrainian territorial integrity, were pressing him to compromise. The result was the first Minsk Protocol, signed on 5 September.

Central to this agreement was an immediate ceasefire, monitored by the OSCE, and the passing of a new law, 'On the Temporary Order of Local Self-Governance in Particular Districts of Donetsk and Luhansk Regions', which would grant a degree of autonomy to the Donbas, early elections and the disarmament and demobilization of 'illegal armed groups'. This proved, however, almost impossible to implement. The Rada was unwilling to grant the rebel regions any special rights until after the Russians had withdrawn and the *opolchentsy* had all laid down their arms; the rebels refused to, as one put it, 'give up our guns and stretch our necks out for the axe' before they had their political concessions. The elections were meant to be carried

Observers from the OSCE Special Monitoring Mission logging the movement of heavy weaponry in eastern Ukraine as part of their withdrawal from the line of contact. Note the unusual 'eyes' on the lead gun. (OSCE Special Monitoring Mission to Ukraine, CC BY 2.0 https://creativecommons.org/licenses/by/2.0, via Wikimedia Commons)

out under the terms of Ukrainian law, but the rebel governments and their Russian allies and masters insisted on carrying them out themselves, without meaningful international monitoring. As for the demobilizations, many of the pro-Maidan volunteer battalions frankly refused to be dissolved. Besides, as most had technically been adopted by the MVS or the ZSU, they argued that they were all legal – even while demanding that the DNR and LNR militias all needed to be disbanded at once. No one trusted anyone else, and no one was willing to make dangerous early concessions.

LITTLE STALINGRAD

The fragile ceasefire that ensued was subject to constant small-scale breaches from both sides, as rival militias probed the others' defences, traded potshots and saw enemy attack in every rustle in the night. The real flashpoint, though, would prove to be Donetsk Airport, which remained in government hands. There had been some suggestion that it might be traded for some settlements under rebel control, but this came to nothing. To Zakharchenko, this was both a humiliation and a practical threat, and he seems to have planned a renewed attempt to capture it, even as he signed the first Minsk Protocol.

DNR forces periodically lobbed shells into the airport complex, not least in the hope of provoking return fire into Donetsk which would justify their propaganda claims about the government's heedlessness of civilian casualties in the Donbas. On the night of 12/13 September, a particularly heavy shelling was followed by an attack from three to five tanks, but was easily repelled. It is unclear whether this was the impromptu initiative of one of the rebel militias or an attempt to probe the defenders' positions. Either way, on the night of 29 September, a full-scale assault was launched by DNR troops drawn from the Oplot, Sparta and Somalia Bns, indirectly supported by Russian regulars, including at least one Orlan-10 reconnaissance drone, which supplemented the targeting information collected from observation posts on nearby high-rise buildings.

What ensued was one of the more epic struggles of the campaign, in which a relative handful of defenders, outnumbered, short on supplies and often heavily outgunned, nonetheless held on to an increasingly devastated airport not for a few days, as Zakharchenko had assumed, but months, earning themselves the nickname 'cyborgs' for their seemingly inhuman tenacity. The airport was defended by fewer than 200 soldiers from the 93rd Mech Bde and the 81st Airmobile Bde's 90th Separate Airmobile Bn, under the 93rd's commander, Col. Oleg Mikats. They had a handful of T-64B tanks and other

The 'cyborgs' who defended Donetsk Airport became national heroes, even commemorated with these special stamps also showing the ruined control tower. (Post of Ukraine, public domain, via Wikimedia Commons)

Ukrainian 152mm 2S3 SPGs provided crucial heavy fire support for the defenders at Donetsk Airport. (Photo by Brendan Hoffman/ Getty Images)

AFVs, but little in the way of heavy weapons, although they were regularly given fire support by the 93rd Bde's own 122mm 2S1s and 152mm 2S3s.

By 3 October, the DNR forces had managed to seize the eastern part of the main airport buildings, including the older terminal building. Fighters from the Sparta Bn even flooded its basement with petrol to which they then set light, hoping to push out the defenders, with partial success. After a brief pause, they then began to try and push the defenders out of the new terminal to the west, which had been built as part of the preparations for the Euro 2012 football championship shared between Poland and Ukraine.

Despite this, the government forces resisted doggedly, resupplied by occasional drops under fire onto the adjacent runway and supply runs and limited rotation of forces through the village of Pisky, just over 2km west of the airport. As a result, paratroopers from the 95th Airmobile Bde were able to be inserted to make up for casualties and allow the evacuation of the severely wounded. The 'cyborgs' were still launching sporadic raids into the old terminal as of 15 October, while consolidating in the new, as well as holding onto the air traffic control tower farther to the west. The new terminal had originally had seven floors, but artillery bombardments and fire had essentially chewed it down to three, at least one of which was contested.

The DNR trumpeted that it had taken the airport the next day, 16 October, publicizing a photo of its flag hanging from the new terminal, but this was quickly disproved. Indeed, DNR forces soon had to abandon the new terminal to regroup, and the tempo of fighting scaled down for a few days as they licked their wounds and furiously demanded that the Russian troops join the direct fighting. While they did step up their artillery support, including periodic bombardments of Pisky to try and interdict resupply efforts, Maj. Gen. Kuzovlev was still unwilling to commit his troops to what was already becoming known as 'Little Stalingrad'. The DNR troops were themselves beginning to become rather spooked by the level of resistance the government soldiers were putting up, making them increasingly cautious. There followed a month of skirmishes and sniping. After all, this was still a war being fought largely on a small scale, a war of platoons and companies rather than battalions and brigades. While the Russians had deployed several thousand troops to relieve Ilovaisk and stabilize the situation in August, and still had at least 3,000 at their disposal in-country, they continued to hope that they could let this be a war fought by their clients and proxies as far as possible. As a Russian officer who had been in Donetsk at the time recalled, 'we didn't think, we really couldn't imagine, that the *opolchentsy* would have such a tough time taking one airport'.

In the hope of breaking the deadlock, Moscow eventually acceded to Zakharchenko's demands and committed operators from the 3rd Spetsnaz Bde to support another attack, as well as fighters from the Rusich Sabotage and Assault Recon Group and a battery of massive 2S4 Tyulpan 240mm mortars. A new assault was launched on 28 November, and although after three days the attackers paused, it was increasingly clear that even the 'cyborgs' were running out of time. Nonetheless, they held on. In part, the issue was not just the defenders' determination but also the rudimentary nature of the DNR's military machine, which was much more teeth than tail; they had fighters, but not much of a logistical framework to sustain operations. Thus, the battle for the airport often took the form of brief flurries of fighting followed by relative lulls, simply because the militias would expend their ammunition and then spend days or weeks scavenging, begging or otherwise acquiring resupply.

On 10 January, the next assault saw the control tower, which the government forces had been holding on to as both an observation post and also a point from which to retrieve what few supply runs could still make it through Pisky, finally destroyed. For the dwindling complement of 'cyborgs', resupply would become increasingly difficult. On 15 January, Zakharchenko claimed that his men had total control of the airport, but as usual he was jumping the gun. Indeed, on 17 January, Kyiv launched an unexpected counter-attack, whether to retake the airport or at least relieve its defenders. Some 600 soldiers from the 3rd Bn of the 80th Separate Air Assault Bde, the 73rd Naval Special Operations Centre, the 3rd Special Forces Rgt and

A DNR soldier rests amid the wreckage of the destroyed Donetsk Airport. (Photo by Andrew Burton/Getty Images)

Note: gridlines are shown at intervals of 1km (0.62 miles).

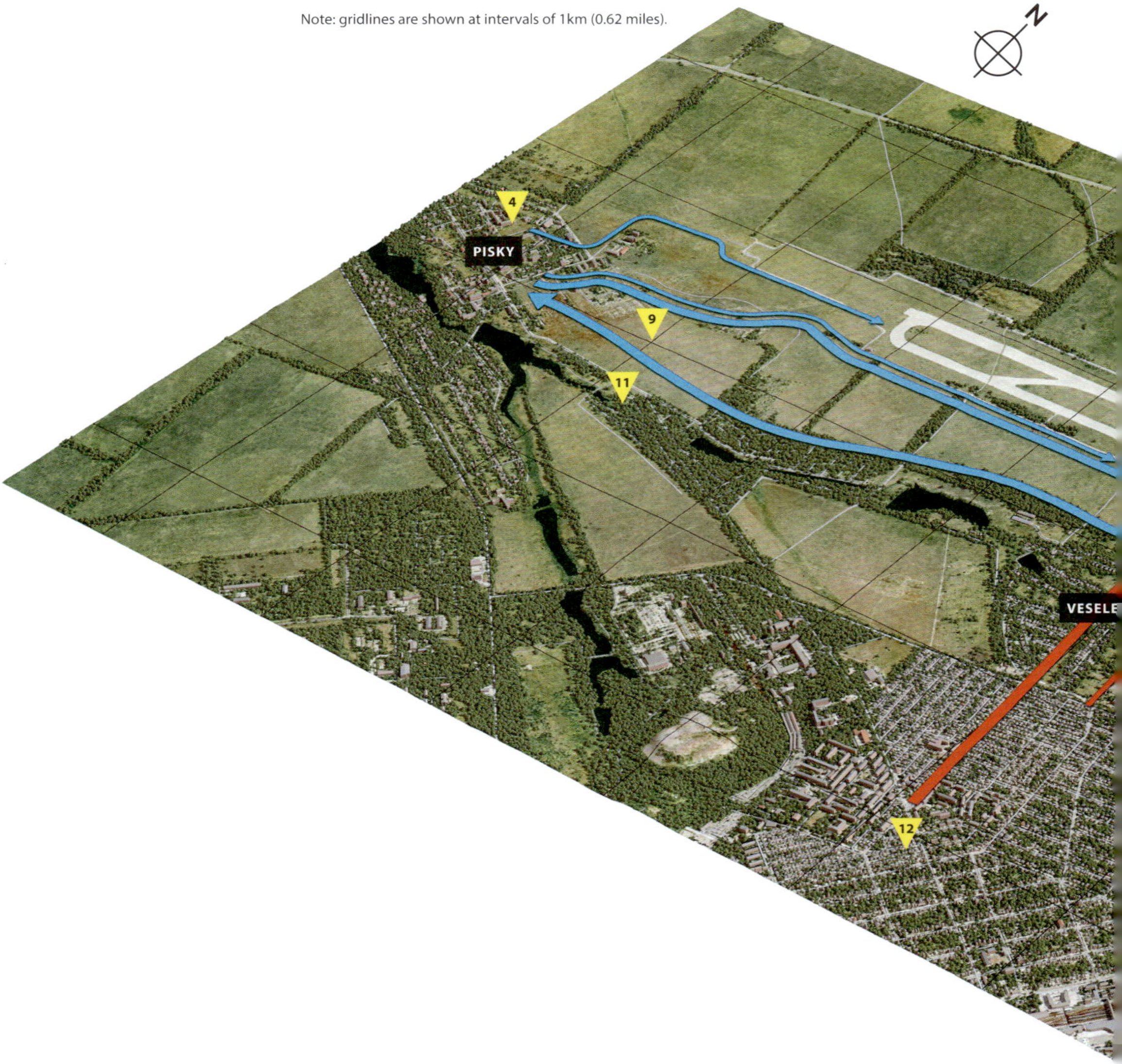

EVENTS

1. 12–13 September: Initial probe (Defenders: Elements of 93rd Mech Bde and the 81st Airmobile Bde)
2. 29 September: First full-scale attack (Elements: Oplot, Sparta and Somalia Bns)
3. 29 September–3 October: DNR forces slowly take old terminal building
4. Defenders reinforced and resupplied through Pisky (Elements: 95th Airmobile Bde)
5. Sporadic government raids into old terminal building
6. 16–23 October: DNR forces establish bridgehead in new terminal, then forced to withdraw
7. 28 November–1 December: New assault launched, with Russian reinforcements (Elements: 3rd Spetsnaz Bde and Rusich Sabotage and Assault Recon Group
8. 10 January: Air traffic control tower finally destroyed in renewed fighting
9. 17 January–20 January: Government counter-attack clears airport (Elements: 80th Separate Air Assault Bde, 73rd Naval Special Operations Centre, 3rd Special Forces Rgt and Right Sector)
10. 17 January: DNR forces destroy Putylivsky bridge
11. Government forces withdraw
12. DNR/Russian forces take airport

THE SECOND BATTLE OF DONETSK AIRPORT, SEPTEMBER 2014–JANUARY 2015

Ultimately, it was inevitable that the rebels would be able to take Donetsk Sergei Prokofiev International Airport. What was unexpected was quite how long it would take, with ferocious resistance by government troops against waves of rebel and later Russian attacks.

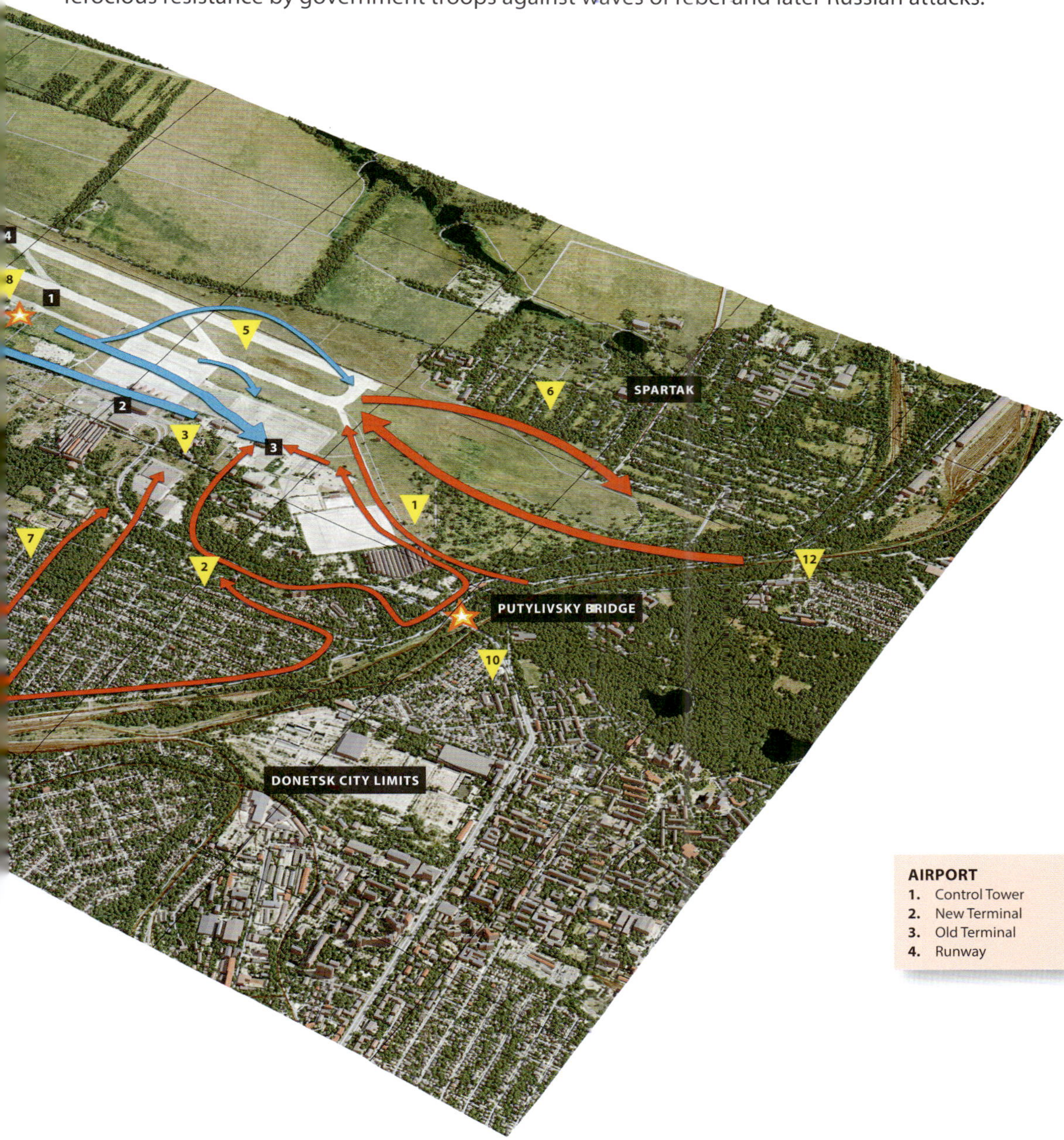

AIRPORT
1. Control Tower
2. New Terminal
3. Old Terminal
4. Runway

Right Sector, approaching through Pisky, caught the attackers by surprise and all but cleared them from the airport. The Putylivsky bridge, connecting the airport to the city, was destroyed to prevent them from advancing farther, although it is not clear if this was a serious risk or whether the DNR leadership simply panicked. Either way, neighbouring regions of Donetsk were hammered by artillery fire, as government and rebel guns staged an artillery duel with 122mm and 152mm cannon and the Russians even passed on a TOS-1 Buratino MLRS for the rebels to use, a formidable weapon firing up to 30 220mm rockets with thermobaric warheads. Ultimately, though, the battered and skeletal remnants of the airport buildings offered too little cover for any longer-term defence and the remaining defenders withdrew in good order to Pisky and thence to Avdiivka. By 22 January, what was left of the airport was in DNR hands.

The 'cyborgs' understandably became something of an icon of national resistance, appearing on t-shirts and murals, in memes and recruitment adverts. They suffered 185 casualties through the whole four-month siege, but according to Kyiv inflicted more than 800 on their enemies (conversely, the DNR rather implausibly claimed that their forces had lost just 43 men). Col. Mikats, who had led the defence to the very end, would then be put in charge of the 169th 'Desna' Training Centre and later in 2015 be promoted to the rank of major general. As he had joined the military only in 1992, this made him the first general in the ZSU who had never served in the Soviet armed forces. Another casualty was the Minsk Protocol. More talks were scheduled in Minsk for 31 January, but the DNR and LNR delegations failed to attend. Zakharchenko simply asserted that the DNR 'will not make any more attempts at ceasefire talks' and will 'advance right up to the borders of the Donetsk region'.

THE BATTLE OF DEBALTSEVE

The struggle over Ilovaisk had highlighted the importance of maintaining strong lines of communication between the DNR and LNR. This, in turn, made the city of Debaltseve all the more important a target for the rebels. It was a strategically vital objective, right on the boundary between Luhansk and Donetsk regions, straddling the railway line and E50/M04 highway between the two capitals. Rebels had seized it in April 2014, but loyalists had

Lt. Gen. Lentsov

Given its increasingly threadbare claims that it was not involved in combat operations in Ukraine, the Russians never released official information about their deployments and commanders. However, when footage was examined of ceasefire negotiations at Debaltseve, Vitaly Kiselyov, deputy commander of the LNR's People's Police, was shown deferring to a burly man in Russian uniform who was quickly identified as Lt. Gen. Alexander Lentsov. A highly decorated officer, Lentsov joined the Soviet paratroopers straight from school, serving as the commander of the 80th Separate Recon Coy of the 103rd Abn Div through a two-year tour in the Soviet war in Afghanistan, before rising to eventually become commander of the 98th Guards Abn Div. He led a peacekeeping detachment in Bosnia and fought in both Chechen wars and the 2008 invasion of Georgia. He was Deputy Commander of the Airborne Forces in 2009–13, then Deputy Commander-in-Chief of the Ground Forces, quietly arriving in the Donbas in September 2014 in the 'Northern Wind' deployments. During the campaign, he reportedly came under fire three times: at Donetsk Airport, on the road to Shyrokyne and near Horlivka.

then recaptured it in July. As a result, it was now at the tip of a 25km salient driving into rebel-held territory.

While battle was still raging around Donetsk Airport (some in Kyiv later claimed that it had been intended as a diversion, but this is unlikely), Moscow decided that Debaltseve had to fall, both for its importance on the ground and also as a warning to Kyiv that it needed to make political concessions before it lost yet more territory. To this end, while rebel troops also played a role, the planning and heavy lifting was in the hands of the Russians, with Lt. Gen. Alexander Lentsov, a well-regarded paratrooper, as their field commander. He mustered a force built around six BTGs and two regiments, making it the largest single concentration of regular Russian forces to date, including eight divisions of rocket and tube artillery (in this context, a division is a three-battery artillery unit, comparable to a regiment), supported by units from both the DNR and LNR, for a total of up to 19,000 soldiers according to Kyiv (only 8,000 according to rebel sources). Against them, Kyiv's forces officially amounted to 4,700 regular Ukrainian troops and 500–700 more from the National Guard, MVS and SBU, although some Russian accounts put them at 8,000 in total. Maj. Gen. Olexander Syrsky, the commander of Section S of the ATO (and one day to become ZSU commander-in-chief) had overall authority for the defence.

On 22 January, in tough winter conditions and supported by a heavy artillery barrage, the Russians and their allies attacked. Debaltseve itself was hit by a hail of shells and rockets, but the ground offensive concentrated on trying to close the neck of the salient. To this end, a BTG from the 28th MR

An artfully shot picture of Lentsov in 2007, then major general and deputy head of the Air Assault Troops, supervising a parachute drop. (Russian Airborne Troops Press Service, CC BY-SA 3.0 https://creativecommons.org/licenses/by-sa/3.0, via Wikimedia Commons)

The remains of a destroyed Ukrainian BMP-2 just outside Vuhlehirsk (Vuglegirsk in the Russian rendition). (Photo by Pierre Crom/Getty Images)

Debaltseve (January–February 2015) orders of battle

Many of these units were represented in the fighting only by smaller elements, and this order includes every unit involved, not all of which were necessarily present throughout the whole engagement.

UKRAINIAN
17th Separate Tank Bde
25th Abn Bde
30th Mech Bde
57th Separate Mot Inf Bde
79th Airmobile Bde
80th Separate Air Assault Bde
92nd Separate Mech Bde
95th Airmobile Assault Bde
128th Separate Mountain Inf Bde
101st Separate Guard Bde of the General Staff
140th Special Forces Rgt
13th Separate Mot Inf Bn
25th Separate Mot Inf Bn
40th Separate Mot Inf Bn
43rd Separate Mot Inf Bn
54th Separate Recon Bn
73rd Naval Special Operations Centre
44th Separate Artillery Bde
26th Separate Artillery Bde
1129th AA Missile Rgt
703rd Engineer Rgt
13th Chernihiv TDB
25th Kievska Rus TDB
40th 'Kryvbas' TDB
42nd Rukh Oporu TDB
National Guard's 1st 'Kulchitsky' Bn
Kyiv-2 Special Purpose Police Bn
Svityaz Special Purpose Patrol Police Coy
Donbas Bn
Dudayev Bn

REBEL
1st Separate MR Bde (DNR)
Kalmius Bde (DNR)
Oplot Bn (DNR)
1st Platov Cossack Rgt (LNR)
Odessa Special Purpose Bde (LNR)
Prizrak Bde (LNR)

RUSSIAN
20th Separate MR Bde
21st Separate MR Bde
28th Separate MR Bde
32nd Separate MR Bde
138th Separate MR Bde
200th Separate MR Bde
13th Tank Rgt of 4th Tank Div
104th Abn Assault Rgt of 76th Abn Assault Div
217th Guards Abn Rgt
232nd Rocket Artillery Bde
45th Abn Spetsnaz Rgt
25th Spetsnaz Bde

Bde struck at the Troitske–Almazna–Popasna triangle on the eastern edge of the neck, pushing aside elements of the 40th Separate Motorized Infantry (Mot Inf) Bn to make worryingly quick gains. Meanwhile, hoping to help close the neck from the west and threaten the M03 road towards Debaltseve, the DNR's Oplot Bde tried to repeat the process near Svitlodarsk. It was nowhere near as successful, though, and was pushed back by the 13th Separate Mot Inf Bn. A Russian BTG based on the 138th Guards MR Bde suffered sufficient losses that it had to be replaced with another from the 27th Guards MR Bde and the 217th Guards Abn Rgt (from the 98th Guards Abn Div).

Nonetheless, the defenders were not only outnumbered but also outgunned, especially as the Russians were using more drones than usual to spot for their long-range artillery, with the 220mm BM-27 Uragan MLRSs proving especially deadly to concentrations of Ukrainian troops. With batteries emplaced around the salient at Nizhny Krynka, Torez, Fashchivka, Stakhanov, Bryanka, Alchevsk and Seleznivka, they were able to hit anywhere within it, and keep up sustained bombardments limited only by their resupply capacity. The 20th and 21st MR Bdes' BTGs led attacks on the village of Vuhlehirsk, west of Debaltseve, to squeeze the salient towards the beleaguered city, while the artillerymen of the DNR's Kalmius Bde demonstrated unusual accuracy in making the roads out of it essentially unusable, with their BM-21 Grad 122mm MLRSs and D-30

122mm howitzers. By 26 January, true to form, Zakharchenko announced that Debaltseve had been surrounded and called on its defenders to lay down their arms. Footage from the beleaguered city, though, gave the lie to his statement and, if anything, more reinforcements from the National Guard and the 57th Mot Inf Bde had been brought into the salient.

Instead, the real focus of active fighting was Vuhlehirsk, and by 28 January, Russian and DNR forces were fighting through its streets. Against them was arrayed a mix of the 13th Separate Mot Inf Bn (largely made up of mobilized reservists), an AT battery of the 42nd Mot Inf Bn and the Svityaz Special Purpose Patrol Police Coy, although they were soon reinforced by a battalion from the 30th Separate Mech Bde. The Ukrainians were forced to withdraw, not least as MT-12 Rapira 100mm AT guns were used against buildings sheltering remaining defenders, and the attackers also called in low-flying Su-25 attack aircraft, which saturated their positions with S-5 55mm rockets. The last Ukrainian troops out, the Svityaz Coy and the 8th Coy of the 30th Bde, left booby-traps in the village and mines on the road back to Debaltseve, but these were inevitably quickly emplaced and in due course would be removed by Russian combat engineers.

In the hope of retaking it before the Russians had had a chance to consolidate their grip, the 25th Separate Mot Inf Bn and the National Guard's Donbas and 1st 'Kulchitsky' Bns made an effort to retake Vuhlehirsk later on the 30th. It started with promise, with the outskirts of the town being surveilled by drones operated by the 73rd Naval Special Operations Centre, after which a company from the Donbas Bn moved into its eastern neighbourhood. There it walked into a trap laid by the Russians, and while the National Guardsmen were able to destroy a tank and a BMP-2 IFV, they were forced to withdraw under fire. The next morning, after an artillery barrage, a new attack was made on Vuhlehirsk. A battalion of the 30th Separate Mech Bde along with the Donbas and 1st 'Kulchitsky' Bns attacked from two directions, the east and the south-west. The latter thrust managed to push to the centre of the city while Russian fire concentrated on the other assault. However, on hearing that a 15-tank column – likely a reinforced mechanized company with added tank platoon – was moving to block their rear, the government forces were pulled out of Vuhlehirsk. The other attack, which had been bogged down in a ferocious hail of tank, machine gun and AGL fire, also withdrew.

Efforts were made to reinforce both Debaltseve and the remaining strongholds keeping the salient's neck open, but there simply were not forces to spare, especially given the need not to leave other targets open to attack. While at least a battalion of the 57th Mot Inf Bde was committed, for example, the bulk had to be kept protecting the Horlivka front, lest it be almost undefended. It was a mark of the desperation for troops that even a company of the 101st Separate Guard Bde of the General Staff, a unit based in Kyiv and primarily charged with the security of military facilities in the capital, had been deployed to the defence of the salient under its commander, Col. Mykola Shvets.

By 3 February, the Russians were concentrating their efforts on Ridkodub, a village south-east of Debaltseve that was at the centre of the deployments of Ukraine's 128th Mountain Inf Bde under Col. Serhy Shaptala, in order to contract their perimeter around the city. It was a mark of just how important holding this was that the brigade was quickly reinforced by two companies

THE BATTLE FOR VUHLEHIRSK, 28 JANUARY 2015 (PP.78–79)

The town of Vuhlehirsk was all but destroyed in the battle for the Debaltseve pocket. Here, two fighters from the DNR's 1st Separate MR Bde and what looks like an operator from the Russian 25th Spetsnaz Bde shelter behind a BTR-82A APC from the 21st Separate MR Bde as they fight their way through the town. The two rebel fighters show the usual mismatched kit and uniforms of most DNR troops at this time. One **(1)** carries a 7.62mm AKM-47 rifle, the other **(2)** – a Cossack by his appearance – a 5.45mm AKS-74U assault carbine, a handy weapon at close quarters but hardly ideal in most combat environments. The Spetsnaz **(3)** carries a modern AKM-74 rifle fitted with a 40mm GP-30 grenade launcher. As was usual at this stage of the conflict, neither the Russian soldier nor the APC have any telltale insignia, but the nature of the equipment gives them away as Russian. A soldier from Ukraine 13th Separate Mot Inf Bn **(4)** lies dead to the left, while overhead, a Russian Su-25 Grach (Rook) attack aircraft **(5)** makes a low pass over the town.

101st Brigade

The 101st Bde for the Protection of the General Staff had been established in 1992 as a successor to the Red Army's 368th Protection and Service Bn, which provided physical protection for the headquarters of the old Kiev Military District. It originally comprised a security battalion, a guard of honour, a band, a C2 (command and control) battalion and the 30th Automobile Transport Base, and was expanded with the addition of two more security battalions in 1995, although it would later lose one of them to the cuts made under Yanukovych. Each security battalion was made up of one mechanized company in BTR-80 APCs, two motorized ones in trucks and GAZ-66s, and a scout platoon.

from the 17th Separate Tank Bde, a battery of 122mm guns and a mortar battery from the 14th Separate Mech Bde. Furthermore, two Mi-24 gunships and an Mi-8 assault helicopter flew strikes against the Russian and rebel forces assembling near the village of Sanzharivka, even if an infuriated report from the 128th Bde's forward air observers records that their ordnance actually landed a kilometre away from their target.

THE DEBALTSEVE CAULDRON

Meanwhile, international concern about the civilians inside the salient was mounting, with electricity and water supplies cut and fighting concentrating on settlements. UN Secretary-General Ban Ki-moon called on the combatants to agree a ceasefire, and as a result a 24-hour truce was agreed in which more than 5,000 civilians were able to leave safely, leaving Debaltseve almost empty of anyone but soldiers. The fighting resumed early on 5 February, though, again concentrating on Ridkodub. A series of entrenched platoon fighting positions had been set up around the village and one to the south known as Stanislav-128 became pivotal. Light infantry from the LNR's Prizrak Bde had already begun to infiltrate the village from the north by

Rebel BM-21 Grad (Hail) MLRSs firing a volley of 122mm rockets during the Debaltseve operation. (Photo by Pierre Crom/Getty Images)

4 February, and Stanislav-128, which was manned by a platoon from the 128th Mountain Bde was effectively isolated, any routes for resupply or withdrawal covered by Russian or rebel fire. Twice, attempts to provide food and ammunition were ambushed, so on 5 February, a concerted effort was made to relieve Stanislav-128 and drive the attackers from Ridkodub by the Donbas Bn's 2nd Coy, in a column led by a T-64 tank and two BMP-2s. They came under heavy mortar and artillery fire and stalled, though, so the operation was pushed back to the next morning. This time, the scout platoon of the 128th Bde and commando platoons from both the 73rd Naval Special Operations Centre and the 140th Special Forces Rgt took the lead, successfully evacuating Stanislav-128 and reaching the village. An assault group from the 30th Bde held Stanislav-128 but the plan had been that two more companies would then join the operation to clear the village. For unclear reasons – the official line is communication difficulties, but allegations of outright cowardice spread – they failed to deploy, and so after six hours Stanislav-128 had to be abandoned, and with it the attempt to retake Ridkodub. While Kyiv deployed Mi-8 assault helicopters, despite the AA threat and poor winter visibility, in an attempt to stave off the inevitable, by 7 February, Ridkodub was firmly in the attackers' hands. In the usual pattern, the assault was conducted largely by Russians, with separatists (in this case the LNR's Prizrak Bde) then securing it afterwards. Many of the tales of human rights abuses connected with the operation were levelled not at the Russian regulars, but these *chistka* (clean-up) operations by the rebels.

Two days later, with the fall of Lohvynove, north of Debaltseve, one of the last routes used to keep the city supplied was cut. A reinforced company each of the 79th and 95th Airmobile Bdes and the 54th Separate Recon Bn, supported by the 13th Chernihiv TDB and commandos from the 3rd Special Forces Rgt – altogether close to a regimental-size deployment, unusually large at this stage of the war – launched an immediate counter-attack, but this failed, not least under renewed bombardment. Although the advance guard, from the 79th Bde, did reach the outskirts of the village, the density of mines and improvised explosive devices was such that they could scarcely

An evocative picture of rebel fighters riding tanks of the DNR's Diesel Bn towards battle at dusk. (Photo by Pierre Crom/Getty Images)

The battle of Debaltseve, January–February 2015

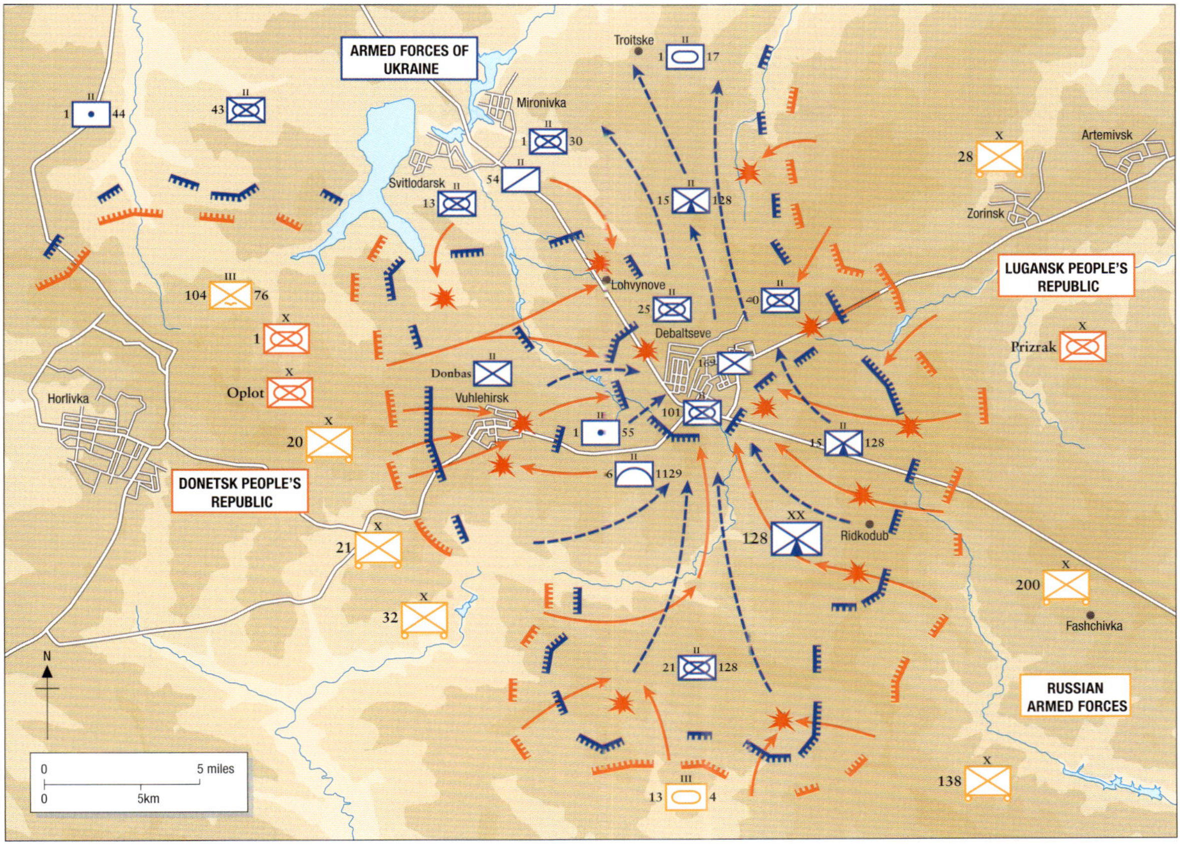

move farther. By this time, Russian counter-attacks were increasing in density and strength. A T-64 tank crew under Lt. Vasyl Bozhok managed to destroy three Russian T-72s in a rearguard operation to cover the paratroopers of the 79th Bde, earning him the gold star of a Hero of Ukraine, but in the main, the arithmetic of battle was against the government forces. By the end of the day, a planned counter-attack had turned into a desperate defensive operation to prevent further Russian advances. A GMZ-2 armoured minelayer hurriedly scattered TM-62 AT mines across the road leading out of Lohvynove, while the nine T-64BM Bulats of the 1st Separate Tank Bde's 3rd Coy began digging in behind this line. A couple of UMP remote minelaying systems on truck chassis spread PTM-3 AT mines to their flanks. Meanwhile, four BM-27 MLRSs and four MSTA-S 152mm SPGs were allocated to cover this last-ditch defence by what was designated the *Bars* (Leopard) tactical group.

Part of its mission was also to keep open the last 'road of life' supply route to Debaltseve. This would, however, prove increasingly difficult, as the Russians did not physically have to block it, simply make sure they kept it under fire control: monitored by scouts and drones such that any convoys could then be disrupted with long-range artillery fire. As well as the usual systems, this also saw the Russians using 2S7 Pion 203mm SPGs, beasts with a 38km unassisted range, 48km when using rocket-assisted shells. Kyiv

The Chechen revenge

The brutal suppression of Chechnya's attempt to wrench itself from Moscow's control in the First (1994–96) and Second (1999–2009) Chechen Wars led to an outflow of defeated fighters, both nationalists and Islamic extremists. Just as many had supported Georgia during its brief war with Russia in 2008, the conflict in the Donbas offered an opportunity for revenge – a very powerful motivator in Chechen culture. Two all- or predominantly Chechen units fought in the Donbas. Arguably the most important was the Dzhokar Dudayev Bn, named for the Chechens' erstwhile independent leader. It emerged from émigré circles in Denmark and was formed at the end of March, under Isa Munayev, who had commanded the defence of the Chechen capital, Grozny, in 1999. It was formed of two light companies, and fought at both Ilovaisk and Debaltseve, where Munayev was killed. In October, a separate unit, the Sheikh Mansur Chechen Peacekeeping Bn split from the Dudayev Bn. Ostensibly, this was just for practical reasons, but the Mansur Bn (really more of a company in size) was from the first regarded as more extreme, and it would be dogged by accusations of human rights abuses. It refused to subordinate itself either to the ZSU or MVS, instead for a while aligning itself with Right Sector's Ukrainian Volunteer Corps.

continued to express optimism, asserting that Debaltseve was still being resupplied regularly and the city was being turned into a fortress. Behind the scenes, though, the mood was much more downbeat. Resupply was proving an increasing problem, with some small loads of ammunition and other consumables being sneaked in through back roads or very occasional – and risky – airdrops.

The soldiers in Debaltseve were tired, while many of the volunteers' skills were not the equal of their fighting spirit. As exhaustion grew, in part due to regular night-time bombardments, friendly fire incidents proliferated.

A T-72 tank and BMP-2 of the DNR's Oplot Bde (which had just been formally expanded from a battalion), advance through Vuhlehirsk. (Photo by Pierre Crom/Getty Images)

The Ukrainians assayed one more counter-attack to try and force a supply convoy through Lohvynove, coordinating a push from outside Vuhlehirsk by the 30th Bde with a sally from Debaltseve itself. When this failed, though, the writing was on the wall for Debaltseve and the whole salient.

The Russian-led offensive had essentially surrounded Debaltseve, but meanwhile, just as Ilovaisk had in many ways forced Kyiv into accepting the first Minsk Protocol, so too this one had helped force a second round of talks to a conclusion of sorts. It was agreed that government forces would withdraw, although given the Ilovaisk experience, not only did Kyiv demand the presence of observers this time, and refuse to abandon its armoured vehicles and heavy weapons, but when its forces withdrew from Debaltseve itself, they moved in relatively small contingents along two separate road routes (Debaltseve–Novohrygorivka–Troitske and Debaltseve–Novohrygorivka–Nyzhne Lozove–Luhansk), having actually set up three in order to have one 'dummy' as a diversion. They comprehensively destroyed the railway lines and other strategic infrastructure of the city then began their withdrawal on 15 February, with the 1st Separate Tank Bde and 30th Mech Bde covering the retreat. Although there were skirmishes along the way, in the main this unfolded as planned.

On the afternoon of 17 February, DNR forces rolled into Debaltseve. True to their attempt to minimize their own role, the Russians let their proxies take the glory. Oplot and the 1st MR Bde occupied all but the western parts of the city, where the last of the defenders were still preparing to withdraw. There appears to have been some sporadic shooting between them, but this was small scale and unplanned. By the next day, the last government troops had left and the salient was being rolled up, with DNR and LNR forces following behind the withdrawing columns and taking village after village. According to the Ukrainian General Staff of Ukraine, almost 2,500 men were eventually extricated from Debaltseve itself, along with 15 tanks and 50 IFVs, while 179 men had died through the whole operation, compared with almost 3,000 rebels and Russian regulars. Needless to say, their enemies painted a different picture, an LNR source claiming that they had lost only 500 men to the loyalists' 2,000. The actual butcher's bill was probably over 250 dead or missing for the government and around 850 for the attackers.

The new front line stabilized along the Luhan River, from east of Horlivka to Sokolohirsk, 60km west of Luhansk. The official Ukrainian after-action report puts a positive gloss on the battle, claiming that 'having eliminated the Debaltseve salient, the Russian-terrorist troops aimed to develop the offensive and capture Artemivsk, Kramatorsk, and, later, Kharkiv' but that 'by steadfastly defending the occupied lines and positions of our troops' it was possible to exhaust the attackers and 'to thwart their plan'. Others

An unusually well-equipped rebel fighter – perhaps a Russian soldier – among the first into Debaltseve. (Photo by Pierre Crom/Getty Images)

were less impressed. Semyon Semenchenko, commander of the Donbas Bn, who had himself been wounded in the fighting for Vuhlehirsk, recognized the 'high heroism of the soldiers and officers of the army, the National Guard and the police battalions'. (Kyiv handed out almost 830 state and ministry medals and awards, 136 of them posthumous.) However, he contrasted that with 'the gross miscalculations of the General Staff and the ATO leadership' including 'disregard for intelligence, lack of normal coordination, [and a] lack of reserves'. Probably the most balanced assessment came from Yuri Biryukov, an aide to the defence minister: 'I don't know if the operation near Debaltseve could have been carried out better, but it certainly could have been carried out worse. Assessing the number of losses in the current conditions and knowing how many enemy forces were there, I think that this is far from the most disastrous operation in the history of the Armed Forces of Ukraine.'

STALEMATE

In December 2015, Putin finally admitted that there were Russians in the Donbas for 'resolving various issues' but, even then, he denied they were combat forces. After all, when it could, Moscow continued to rely on its proxy militias, albeit increasingly under Russian officers. However, despite efforts to build them into a serious conventional army, they were often undisciplined or simply outgunned. Whenever government forces looked as if they were likely to make serious gains, though, the Russians surged in their

Ukraine's politics would remain turbulent until the Russian invasion in 2022 brought a new mood of national unity. Here Donbas Bn soldiers stand guard outside parliament. (Photo by Anatolii Stepanov/Anadolu Agency/Getty Images)

battalion tactical groups to turn the tide. Nonetheless, a kind of bloody and dynamic stalemate was in the works. The front lines might ebb and flow, but unless Moscow was ready for a full-scale war, its proxies could not secure the Donbas. On the other hand, as long as Moscow was willing to bail them out, nor could Kyiv's forces, even as they become more competent and confident, crush the DNR and LNR.

The fighting at Donetsk Airport had already led to a renewed flurry of diplomatic activity, and it had become painfully clear just how irrelevant the original Minsk Protocol had become. As a result, François Hollande and Angela Merkel presented a new peace plan on 7 February following separate negotiations with Poroshenko and Putin. Another summit was held in Minsk on 11 February, although the talks were difficult and lengthy. After 16 hours of shuttle diplomacy (as Poroshenko would not directly meet with Zakharchenko and Plotnitsky, meaning everything had to be handled through intermediaries), a new package of measures was agreed. It was not, to be blunt, much of an improvement on Minsk I, hastily written and ambiguous, but by this stage exhaustion and the French and German leaders' desperation not to leave with nothing had set in. The new Minsk II package envisaged a ceasefire monitored by the OSCE, the withdrawal of heavy weapons from the front line, prisoner swaps and again greater rights for the Donbas in return for elections, as well as amnesties for everyone involved in the rebellion.

The ceasefire, which came into force on 15 February but took several days really to apply (and was fudged around the ongoing fighting in Debaltseve), was at least in theory relatively straightforward. The withdrawal of heavy weapons was a more complex operation. The idea was to create a security zone along the front line, with artillery pulled 25km from the line of contact, most MLRSs 35km and the most powerful MLRSs and tactical missile systems fully 70km. The OSCE was meant to monitor all this, as well as the ceasefire, using teams on the ground and drones in the air. At the same time, 'all foreign armed formations' and 'mercenaries' were meant to leave Ukrainian territory.

The political problems, though, were as numerous as they were intractable. Moscow was not going to abandon the DNR and LNR unless and until it knew that they were so tightly bound back into the Ukrainian political system that Russia had its proxies at the heart of the government. The DNR and LNR leaders, many of whom had built for themselves lucrative criminal empires, preferred to be big fish in small ponds. Kyiv was not going to let them legitimize themselves and welcome them into the new Ukrainian political establishment while they kept their private armies. As for the Ukrainian nationalists, they flatly rejected the whole deal. Right Sector's Dmytro Yarosh said that his Ukrainian Volunteer Corps would continue fighting 'until complete liberation of Ukrainian lands from Russian occupiers'. Nonetheless, by later in February, some progress was being made on both sides towards pulling back their heavy artillery, and the tempo of combat operations did slacken. However, the law that the Rada passed on elections in the Donbas turned out not to be what the Russians, DNR and LNR had expected, and the latter denounced it as a 'one-sided' modification of what had been agreed. Instead, a decision was eventually made to go ahead with elections independent of Kyiv's laws and scrutiny, which Poroshenko in turn denounced as illegitimate. The fighting had diminished, for now, and the initial campaign of the undeclared war was over, but there had been no meeting of minds, no true basis for peace.

The DNR and LNR after Minsk II, 2015

AFTERMATH

There was no real aftermath, as such. After Minsk II, the conflict may have subsided somewhat, but was still subject to periodic flare-ups and escalations, especially (but not solely) on the side of the DNR and LNR. Moscow would neither formally annex the rebel pseudo-states nor cut them loose – it really just saw them as a political weapon against Kyiv. The result was a seemingly unresolvable cycle of on-off ceasefires, trench warfare, sporadic local fighting, mutual sniping and shelling, and equally mutual recrimination. In this respect, the slide to full-scale war between Russia and Ukraine in 2022 was perhaps, in hindsight, inevitable.

The graves of unknown fighters identified only by number at Mospyne cemetery. (Photo by Pierre Crom/Getty Images)

BANDIT KINGDOMS

It was always something of caricature, but there was also some basis to the widespread Ukrainian stereotype that 'every third man in the Donetsk region is in prison, has been in prison, or will be in prison'. Much of the Donbas was impoverished and industrial, crime levels were relatively high, and there were more prisons there than anywhere else in the country (20 in Donetsk and 16 in Luhansk), and many rootless ex-convicts simply remained there on release. During the early stages of the insurrection, many street gangs and low-level criminals joined the militias on both sides, leading to numerous incidents of looting and worse, but as the pseudo-states became more settled, the scope for more organized criminality increased. Leaders in both the LNR and DNR developed criminal empires based on embezzlement and corruption, and while there may have been a war on, until 2022, Ukrainian and Russian organized crime networks cooperated freely through the Donbas region, smuggling everything from Afghan heroin to Chinese-made counterfeit goods to Europe.

Smuggling also became central to the pseudo-states' economies. Moscow was unwilling to bankroll them fully, but instead turned a blind eye as, to balance the books, both of them developed massive, institutionalized criminal operations. The largest was the smuggling of sanctioned Donbas coal across the border, where it would be – for want of a better word – 'laundered' by mixing it with Russian coal and sold on international markets. Indeed, the irony was that Ukraine was a major consumer of this black-market coal, in the process helping sustain the unrecognized pseudo-states fighting against it.

UKRAINE ARMING

Meanwhile, living in the shadow of potential future Russian aggression, Ukraine was forced to prepare for war. In 2018, Kyiv would adopt new language, calling the rebel areas 'Temporarily Occupied Territories' and replacing the term ATO with 'Joint Forces Operation'. What may sound like meaningless wordplay did have practical significance. It wrote out of the record the (limited but genuine) extent to which the original insurrections, at least, had reflected serious local concerns, not just Russian manipulation. It also coincided with a more assertive line from the government forces. They had already begun episodically trying to nudge their positions forward, deeper into the so-called 'grey zone', the no-man's-land along the line of contact. They realized that this could not be converted into a serious attempt to roll back the rebel lines, though, without triggering a Russian response.

Meanwhile, the ZSU was rearming, especially with Western assistance, and full NATO membership was again a priority. Having inherited a structure, doctrine and officer corps still very much shaped by their Soviet legacy, increasingly the Ukrainians looked West, instead, with everything from new uniforms to an even greater enthusiasm for joint operations and exercises. Efforts locally to licence-produce the Swedish Saab JAS 39 Gripen fighter foundered on a lack of funds, but while it still depended on dwindling stocks of Soviet-era airframes, the air force was at least able to step up live flying in training and recertification. As for the navy, it began to rebuild

The experiences of the Donbas campaign brought a new commitment to rearmament, closer integration with NATO and expanded foreign assistance, such that, by 2022, the Ukrainian armed forces were in far better shape to resist invasion. (Photo by Maxym Marusenko/NurPhoto via Getty Images)

with smaller vessels geared more toward coastal defence and denial, with the first two of a series of Gyurza-M-class artillery boats in service by the end of 2016.

The ZSU was also gradually expanded. By 2016, the Ground Forces had grown to 169,000, and this would reach 215,000 by 2022, with some 900,000 reservists. That same year, the Air Assault Forces and Special Operations Forces were both made into standalone arms of service, and in 2018 the former was expanded with the addition of the 132nd Separate Recon Bn. The Naval Infantry Corps was brought up to a strength of three line brigades, with a new base at Mykolaiv and a training academy at Odesa. Beyond numbers and training, the Ukrainians were also planning, working on the assumption that they would be fighting Russia and its proxies, whether Moscow initiated it or because Kyiv decided forcibly to bring the rebel Donbas back under its control. So they watched the evolution of the Russian military and planned and wargamed potential conflict scenarios, preparations which stood them in good stead in 2022.

THE SLIDE TO WAR

Putin would prove unwilling to abandon his efforts to, as he saw it, bring Kyiv back into the fold. He was not interested in annexing Novorossiya – for all his talk about concern for the Russian-speaking Ukrainians – but instead in trying to force Kyiv to take back the DNR and LNR, but with so much autonomy that not only would Moscow's proxies be able to stay

The Donbas, April 2022

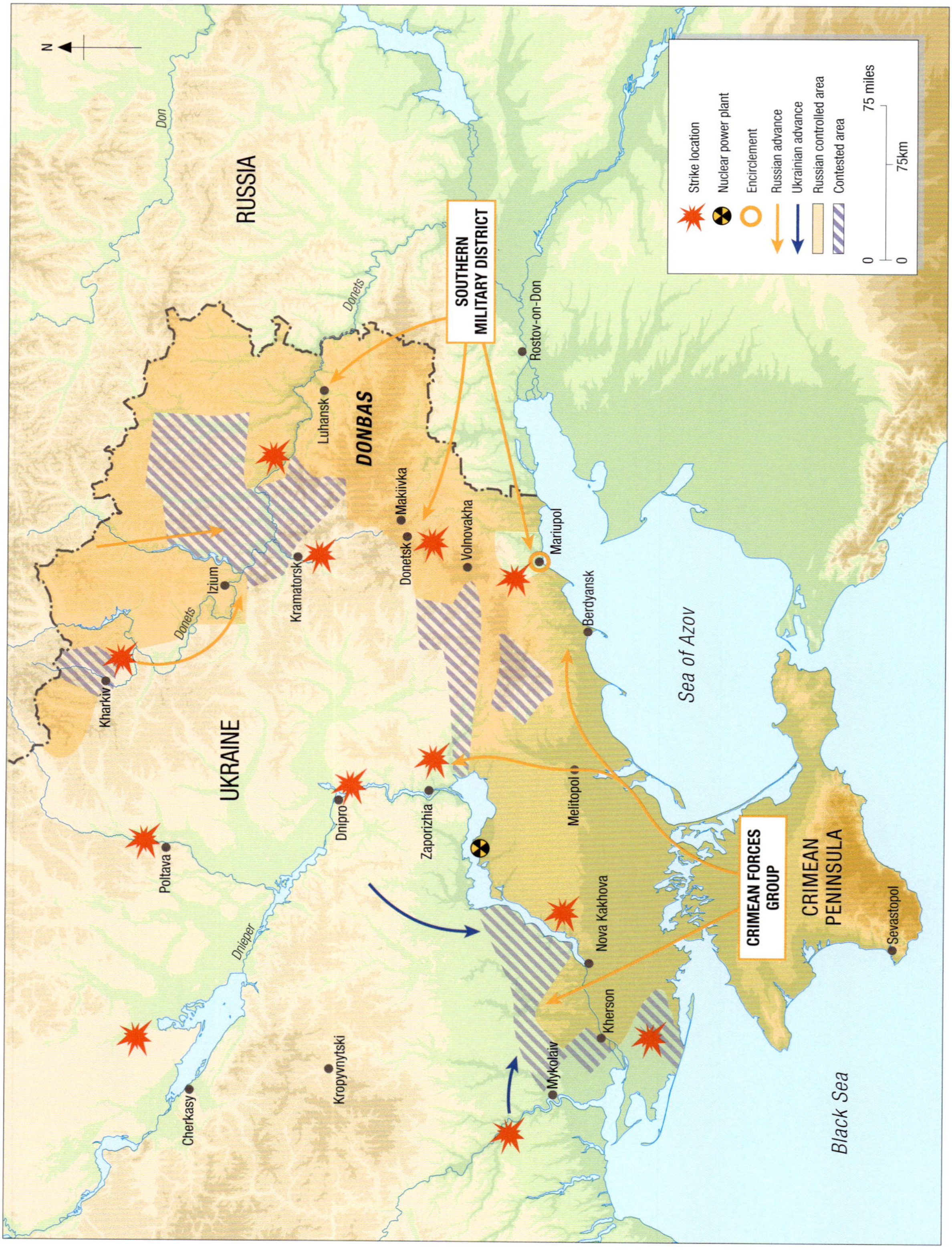

in power, they would have a virtual veto on government policy. As first Poroshenko and then, after his election in 2019, Volodymyr Zelensky were unwilling to take in such an obvious Trojan Horse, Putin became increasingly exasperated. In 2021, he tried military intimidation, building up a large army on Ukraine's borders to try and force Kyiv to make concessions.

Although arguably this might have succeeded, had Putin kept up the pressure, by February 2022 he finally decided on more direct methods. Reassured by his compliant spy chiefs that the Ukrainians would welcome, or at least accept, the imposition of some Moscow-friendly new regime, and that any resistance would be limited, he decided to invade.[3] In the process, he embroiled Russia in the most serious war it had fought since the collapse of the USSR. Yet arguably this was just the culmination of the undeclared intervention into the Donbas in 2014, when Putin committed himself to forcing Kyiv back into Russia's sphere of influence, in the process setting himself against the inexorable rise of Ukrainian nationhood.

The lack of a long-term resolution to the Donbas conflict contributed to the 2022 full-scale invasion. Here, Ukrainian artillery fires on Russian positions outside the then-contested city of Bakhmut in November 2022. (Photo by BULENT KILIC/AFP via Getty Images)

3 See Raid 62, *Kyiv 2022: The battle for Ukraine's capital*

FURTHER READING

Arutunyan, Anna, *Hybrid Warriors: Proxies, Freelancers and Moscow's Struggle for Ukraine*, Hurst (2022)

Cohen, Michael, 'Ukraine's Battle at Ilovaisk, August 2014: The Tyranny of Means', *Military Review* (June 2016)

Galeotti, Mark, *Putin's Wars: From Chechnya to Ukraine*, Osprey (2022)

Gubarev, Pavel, *Fakel Novorossii* [*The Torch of Novorossiya*], Piter (2015)

Howard, Colby & Ruslan Pukhov (eds), *Brothers Armed: Military Aspects of the Crisis in Ukraine*, 2nd edition, EastView (2015)

Kofman, Michael et al, *Lessons from Russia's Operations in Crimea and Eastern Ukraine*, RAND (2017)

Laryš, Martin, *Rebel Militias in Eastern Ukraine: From Leaderless Groups to Proxy Armies*, Routledge (2025)

Marples, David (ed), *The War in Ukraine's Donbas: Origins, Contexts, and the Future*, Central European University Press (2021)

Matveeva, Anna, *Through Times of Troubles: Conflict in Southeastern Ukraine Explained From Within*, Lexington (2018)

Noorman, Randy, 'The Battle of Debaltseve: A Hybrid Army in a Classic Battle of Encirclement' *Small Wars Journal* 17 (2020)

Plokhy, Serhii, *The Russo-Ukrainian War: The Return of History*, W. W. Norton & Co. (2023)

Sanders, Deborah, 'Ukraine's Third Wave of Military Reform 2016–2022: Building a Military Able to Defend Ukraine Against the Russian Invasion', *Defence & Security Analysis*, vol. 39, no. 3 (2023)

Vovk, Irina, *Donet'skii Aeroport: Spravzhnya Istoriya* [*Donetsk Airport: The True History*], Folio (2022)

INDEX

Figures in **bold** refer to illustrations.